"CONNECT is made to order for people hoping to climb the ladder of success—it is detailed in every facet that can help you move forward in your personal and professional life."
—*Dick Vitale, ESPN and ABC sports analyst*

"There is nothing more foundational to success in every area of life than *connection*. Whether in business, family, or personal health and well-being, connection breeds good things and disconnection breeds destruction. This book gives us a very useful map for essential points of connection that we need in our organizations, our families, our relationships, and our personal lives. I was reminded, and inspired, and you will be too."
—*Dr. Henry Cloud, bestselling author,* Boundaries

"Keith Harrell's energy and experience as a corporate trainer and motivational speaker have given him a unique insight into how high-performing individuals and organizations operate. CONNECT offers a fresh perspective and powerful approach to personal and organizational transformation, I have seen it work and now there's a book to make it possible."
—*Michael Hinojosa Ed.D., superintendent, Dallas Independent School District*

"CONNECT is a masterpiece that clearly demonstrates why Keith Harrell and Hattie Hill can help every business to grow faster and allow the dedicated people in every business to become as successful as they are willing to allow themselves to be."
—*Ben Cornett, president, Honeywell Security*

"CONNECT is an impressive and powerful work that brilliantly introduces key success principles, which, if applied, will wonderfully transform your life."
—*S. Charles Murray, United States administrative law judge, colonel, United States Army (Retired)*

"Having experienced Keith 'Dr. Attitude' Harell's pearls of positive attitude and put them into practice, I found myself totally absorbed and called to action by his CONNECT: *Building Success Through People, Purpose, and Performance.* It's like having my own personal performance coach. This is a must read for any organization or individual looking to move performance to the next level."
—*Al Policy, president & CEO, CreditFirst*

"Keith Harrell continues to be a trailblazer by advocating how the right attitude raises your altitude in life, professionally and personally. He is the

'evangelist of disciplines' that help us overcome adversity and fear to affect positive change and outcomes. This book will help you deepen your own understanding of how you control your fate."
—*Angie L. Reese-Hawkins, president and CEO, YMCA of Metropolitan Washington*

"One of the best books that I have read in the last decade. Once again, we are reminded that having a compelling positive attitude can truly enable us to have surefire success and build lasting relationships based on a genuine heartfelt connection to create a win-win for all whom we come in contact with."
—*Brad Jones, territory sales director and vice president, Aflac*

"If you want to be a successful manager, CONNECT is the perfect tool to utilize. The subtitle says it all: 'People, Purpose, Performance.' When we connect with the people in the organization we can accomplish great things together."
—*Brett Barrowman, vice president, Conference and Travel Management Services, American Fidelity Assurance Company*

"Wow! I was thoroughly engaged in the reading and immediate impact of CONNECT. Knowing the cardinal rule, that it takes twenty-one days of repetition to form a habit, I believe that this book is the exception to the rule. As I read CONNECT, it challenged my thought process immediately to search for ways of change regarding my family, my career, and just people that I come into contact with in everyday life. The book is universal and everyone that reads it will undoubtedly be changed. As we live in a microwave society what a powerful and refreshing way to re-CONNECT us in life to what is most important: people, purpose, and our performance."
—*Diana Harrison, business manager, Jackson Acura*

"A great way to build employee commitment and increase productivity. It is truly a friendly education that brings about self-awareness (ICARE). It focuses on 'how to,' not philosophy and theory. When embracing the seven CONNECT steps it becomes a roadmap to success in any facet of one's life."
—*Garnett Campbell , vice president, Human Resources, Cox Communications, Inc.*

"In today's fast-paced society and enhanced technology, communications have become too impersonal. CONNECT is a timely and refreshing reminder of the importance of connecting with people in a more direct and personal way. This is a terrific book for everyone—students, parents, managers, and professionals."
—*Gary Wofford, executive director, Association of Taco John's Franchisees, Inc.*

"This book is a must read for any sales professional, whether you are a manager or a bag-carrying sales rep. The message on connecting with your team and connecting with your customer is exactly what we need in today's world of 'sales presentations' versus 'sales calls.' We've lost the power of the connection and need to get it back. If 'Attitude Is Everything,' then the power to CONNECT and the BE-Attitudes are what enable us to harness that Attitude and push through to the next level and beyond."
—*John S. Cooper, executive vice president, North American Sales, SunGard Availability Services*

"'Dr. Attitude' masterfully walks you through his simple, pragmatic, and healthy approach on self-improvement. His 'Seven CONNECT steps' and 'BE-Attitudes' provide principles that each and every one of us can incorporate into both our personal and professional lives to ensure greater success and fulfillment."
—*Jorge Cadenas, finance manager, large midwestern company*

"Keith's unwavering faith and passion to inspire others to greatness leaves you speechless! If you want to reach your full potential, tap into an adventurously successful life, CONNECT is a must read!"
—*Kim Frye, regional sales manager, Times Services, Inc.*

"I have been working with Keith Harrell for more than ten years and was excited to preview his new book on improvng our connections for increased personal and professional achievement. It is filled with practical action steps and inspirational stories to build lasting success. I highly recommend it."
—*Bridgett P. Paradise, General Manager, Human Resources, large software company*

"Keith Harrell has done an excellent job of inspiring the heart, appealing to the head, and motivating the hands into action with this book. I think anyone who is motivated for personal and organizational growth will benefit from these principles and applying them to their professional and personal life."
—*Randy Melville, senior vice president, Frito-Lay Sales*

"CONNECT puts it all into perspective for all of us. He clearly shows how one can boost productivity and retention in the workplace as well as how one can gain a better sense of the work-life balance, which all managers and leaders struggle with, by a strong commitment and a positive attitude. You must first determine what your chemical makeup is and look within yourself. This is a must-read super-fantastic book."
—*Larry Magee, CEO and president of BFS Retail & Commercial Operations, LLC*

"Keith's BE-Attitudes are an essential blue print for achieving both professional and personal success. In the Banking industry, where a focus on customer service and performance is mandatory, the book's concepts are vital. "

—*Alisha Nasse, private banking relationship manager, Georgian Bank*

CONNECT

ALSO BY KEITH HARRELL

*Attitude Is Everything: 10 Life-Changing Steps to
Turning Attitude into Action*

*Attitude Is Everything Workbook: Strategies and Tools for
Developing Personal and Professional Success*

The Attitude of Leadership: Taking the Lead and Keeping It

An Attitude of Gratitude: 21 Life Lessons

Attitude Is Everything for Success: Say It, Believe It, Receive It

ALSO BY HATTIE HILL

Smart Choices That Will Change Your Life

Women Who Carry Their Men

CONNECT

*Building Success Through
People, Purpose, and
Performance*

Keith Harrell

with Hattie Hill

Collins

An Imprint of HarperCollins*Publishers*

CONNECT. Copyright © 2007 by Keith Harrell. All rights reserved. Printed in the United States of America. No part of this book may be used or reproduced in any manner whatsoever without written permission except in the case of brief quotations embodied in critical articles and reviews. For information, address HarperCollins Publishers, 10 East 53rd Street, New York, NY 10022.

HarperCollins books may be purchased for educational, business, or sales promotional use. For information, please write: Special Markets Department, HarperCollins Publishers, 10 East 53rd Street, New York, NY 10022.

FIRST EDITION

Designed by Joseph Rutt

Library of Congress Cataloging-in-Publication Data is available upon request.

ISBN: 978-0-06-124175-8
ISBN-10: 0-06-124175-X

07 08 09 10 11   ID/RRD   10 9 8 7 6 5 4 3 2 1

This book is dedicated to three of my attitude coaches:
Art Berg, Bob Moawad, and Ray Pelletier.

They were blessed and empowered to CONNECT
with millions, making a positive mark that can never be erased.
I thank God for giving me the opportunity to CONNECT
and learn from these three great leaders.
Their legacy lives on.

CONTENTS

CONNECT

INTRODUCTION

I was a senior in high school, standing at the free-throw line at the semifinal game of the state basketball playoffs. The Garfield High School Bulldogs—AKA the "Super Dogs"—had wiped the floor with our opponents all season, but this game had tested our mettle both physically and mentally. We were playing the Lincoln High School "Abes" of Tacoma, Washington, and for some reason we just weren't getting the job done. We'd been behind at half-time, and with four minutes left on the clock Lincoln was up by six points.

Our coach called a time-out, and all the players went to the bench. For the first time in the season, our side felt disorganized and directionless. Coaches were arguing about strategy; players were looking at one another with disbelieving eyes. What had happened to the All-Star team that had accomplished a 22–0 record with such apparent ease?

Something inside me said, *No way are we gonna lose this game!* I stepped into the middle of the coaches and my teammates and I yelled, "Give *me* the ball!"

It was as if a bolt of electricity had shot through the group. In that one moment, the entire team remembered who we were and why we were there. We connected in a way we hadn't done the entire game. The coach looked at all of us; then he said, "Okay, let's do it. Keith gets the ball. Let's go!"

We ran back on that court as one team. I got the ball, shot it, and hit nothing but net—two points. When Lincoln got the ball, we went into a 1–3–1 full court press, with me on the ball. I stole the ball, shot, kissed it off the glass, and made two more. I was in the zone. I could hear our coaches yelling encouragement from the bench. My team felt the shift in energy and pressed hard on defense. We stole the ball again; they passed it to me, and I scored once more. The game was tied.

On the next play I went up for a rebound and was fouled, crashing to the floor hard. I didn't even feel it—all I knew was that now I would have two free throws to put us ahead.

That's the moment when I found myself at the free throw line. The momentum of the game hung on these two shots. If I made them, chances were we would sweep to victory. If I missed, Lincoln would have ample opportunity to drive to the opposite end of the court and score.

I could literally feel every eye in the arena on me. The screams of the Lincoln crowd were unbelievably loud as they tried to distract me. Yet I could still make out the voices of our coaches and the other players on the bench yelling, "Sink it, Silk (my nickname)! You can do it!" The energy and focus that my teammates were sending in my direction were palpable. It was as if every single Garfield player, coach, and fan had their hands on my arm, guiding me as I aimed and shot.

Swish! First one, then another ball went through the net. If I had thought it was loud before, I had no idea—the Garfield fans blew the roof off the arena when they saw us go ahead. We used the remaining time to score five more points, winning the game by seven.

At the final buzzer my teammates and I grabbed one another, hugged, cheered, and high-fived as the other players and coaches from our bench ran out to join us. The Garfield High Super Dogs went on to win the state championship, and since then our victories have inspired subsequent Garfield basketball teams to strive to emulate our success.

Our achievement that day was created by an attitude of teamwork, a common purpose, unending hard work, and a dedication to accomplish our goal no matter what. But more than that, I believe the Garfield Super Dogs demonstrated one of the most vital secrets of achieving success in life: *the power to connect.*

In the years since that high school victory—through college, through fourteen years as a sales executive and then corporate trainer for IBM, and for the past fifteen years as a speaker and author—I have always believed and focused my message on the importance of attitude in creating success. But through the years I've also learned that while attitude is where it starts, "connect" carries attitude out into the world. Our attitude comes from our ability to connect—with ourselves, with our mission, and most important, with other people.

The subtitle of this book is "Building Success through People, Purpose, and Performance." That's because I believe that success happens only when we use our innate drive to connect to fuel those three aspects of our lives. Everyone who succeeds does so through relationships with *people*. Nothing in this world was ever created, built, produced, amassed, fostered, distributed, or utilized without the support of other people. The artist who paints in a studio far from all living souls depends on other people to produce her paints or canvas, to grow the food for her table, to generate the electricity that powers the lights in her studio, and on and on. And eventually her art will most likely find its way to be viewed and, she hopes, appreciated by other people.

In today's interconnected world, most businesses understand that the best way to produce results comes only through bringing people together—employees, customers, and shareholders. When a business connects, it's far easier for that business to weather the ups and downs of the business cycle. Connected employees are more likely to go the extra mile for the business. Connected customers mean referrals and brand loyalty. Connected shareholders aren't likely to file lawsuits at the smallest drop in stock price.

But to create meaningful and lasting success, people and businesses must create emotional links not only with one another but also with a strong uplifting *purpose*. I played basketball for all four years of high school in Seattle. The first two years I felt really connected to my teammates, and of course I wanted us to win. But it wasn't until my junior and senior years that our team connected to the strong and uplifting purpose of winning the metro-city championship. When we united around that purpose my junior year, we nailed the metro-city championship for Garfield for the first time in a decade. Our senior year we expanded our purpose to win it all: holiday, city, regional, and state. That bigger purpose transformed each player as well as the entire team. We performed far better than we ever had because we connected with one another and our common purpose.

When *people* are connected with a strong, uplifting *purpose*, superstar *performance* becomes second nature. And I believe that building that connection between people, purpose, and performance can be accomplished in a clear, simple fashion. When you create and sustain the power to connect, your success is not only possible—it is virtually guaranteed.

CONNECT Is
Your Framework for Success

You are not here to merely make a living.
You are here in order to enable the world to live
more amply, with greater vision,
with a finer spirit of hope and achievement.
—Woodrow Wilson

In my career as a sales executive, corporate trainer, and professional speaker, I have spoken with a lot of people in every kind of industry and company. I'm always asking them, "What kind of training do you need? Why do you want me to speak to your group or come to your company?" And because I'm known as "Dr. Attitude," the answer is almost always the same: "Our folks need to improve their attitude."

"Keith, we've got some great employees and managers, and some really high performance goals," a manager once told me. "But the people just aren't cutting it. They're not getting the job done to the levels that we need. We're missing our targets, and we figure an attitude adjustment could help."

When I looked at the company, I agreed that a lot of the employees had less than great attitudes. "Sure, I can get them motivated, and I can show them how to keep a positive attitude no matter what," I told this manager. "But what are you and the company planning to do with these super-motivated people when I'm done? What kind of training are we going to offer to maintain this level of motivation and success?"

He looked at me in confusion. "What do you mean?" he asked.

"Attitude is only half of the equation," I said. "Performance comes from attitude, but continuous improvement—going from good to better and better to best—is an ongoing process. Your employees have to connect to the company's goals and its mission. They also have to connect to one another and to you as their leader. A great attitude helps make it easier to connect, but all the effort can't come from one side—either the employees or the company.

"You've tried to connect from the company side with performance goals and mission statements and bringing in someone like me," I continued. "But you've got to remember that to connect you need to grab people's hearts, not just their minds. What kind of positive, uplifting relationships are you going to create with your employees so they'll go the extra mile for you? Because that's what it's going to take. Attitude will give them the emotion; but connecting with their team, the company, and the reasons for wanting it to succeed will give them the drive to produce ongoing outstanding results."

As much as we all want to succeed, what we *really* should be striving for is the power to connect. The ability to connect lies at the core of both personal and professional success. When you connect, it's like mixing air into the gasoline in your car. You may think your car runs on gas, but it doesn't. For the gas to make the engine run, it has to be mixed with air before it's fed into the carburetor. That air is connection, and attitude is the spark plug that brings fire to the mixture. When you have the right fuel (the relationship, the purpose, the goal, the idea, etc.) and you add air (connect) to that fuel, then the spark of a winning attitude will supercharge your performance, and it will power you to success.

> The ability to connect is the power that lies at the core of both personal and professional success.

WE'RE BORN TO CONNECT

The drive to connect is part of our DNA. When children are born, they must connect with their mothers for food and care. And we're just talking about physical connection; our need for emotional connection is just as important, if not more important, for our very survival. In fact, if babies don't receive emotional connection from caregivers, they can wither away. It's called failure to thrive syndrome, and it can kill or emotionally cripple babies who grow up in institutions or other situations where they don't receive the love and connection they need.

We'll do almost anything to feel linked to someone else. Did you see the movie *Cast Away*? Tom Hanks' character, Chuck, is marooned on a desert island for seven years. He manages to care for his physical needs—starting a fire, getting food and shelter, and so on. But then he runs up against his biggest challenge: loneliness. He has no one to connect to other than himself. It gets so bad that he paints a face and puts grass "hair" on a volleyball, and he names this companion Wilson. Wilson is his only friend for all the years Chuck is on the island. Chuck talks to Wilson, argues with him, makes up with him, laughs with him— just as if Wilson were a real person. When Chuck finally escapes on a raft, he takes Wilson with him. And when Wilson drifts off the raft while Chuck is sleeping, we see Chuck's unbearable pain when he wakes up and finds his "friend" gone.

Our basic human need to connect can be a force for good or evil. In fact, people will do a lot of really stupid things simply to connect. If you read about kids who get involved with gangs, most of the time it's not because they're attracted to a life of crime. It's not even because they feel more powerful. It's because the gang gives those kids an overwhelming feeling of connection, of being part of something. On the other hand, recent social studies have shown that even in the poorest neighborhoods, strong, positive social connections like the kind provided by church groups, YMCAs, Boys and Girls Clubs, and other organizations can result in lower crime rates, less drug use and teen pregnancy, and better performance in school by kids in the neighborhood.

IT'S ALL TOO EASY TO DISCONNECT

When we connect, we have power and drive. When we feel *dis*-connected, there's a sense of something missing, and a large part of our motivation and inner drive disappears. Today it seems as if we're more disconnected than ever from much of our world. We rarely connect face-to-face, or even voice to voice, anymore without some kind of electronic device being involved. We e-mail, fax, IM, text message, teleconference, or leave voice mails. We shop online, and we spend our evenings playing computer games with online opponents or zoning out in front of the TV. When we're out in public, we're either plugged in to our iPods or talking on our Bluetooth headsets. We don't bother to connect with the people standing right in front of us because we're too busy with our gadgets!

This electronic pseudo-connection makes us feel as if we're linked to other people, but it can cause a kind of emotional starvation. It's like eating fast food: it may taste good in the moment, but it won't nourish you in the long run, and it's no substitute for a real meal. In the same way, all this electronic cross talk can never take the place of the deep personal bonding that human beings crave.

I read a story about a gentleman whose house lost power one evening during an ice storm. He described how he, his wife, and their children left their various computers, TVs, and MP3 players and came together in the den. With nothing else to distract them, the family started playing board games by candlelight. They laughed, talked, shared about their lives, and had a marvelous time. They connected on a personal level. We all want to connect in that way, whether it's with our families, our teammates, our co-workers, or our customers.

JOY COMES WHEN
WE CONNECT

We have opportunities every day to connect. Several years ago I was sitting in the Las Vegas airport waiting for a flight, which had been delayed a second time. I'd been on the road for an entire month, and I was ready to get back *home*! Now, even "Dr. Attitude" can have a bad moment or two, so I'll admit I was sitting in that airport feeling sorry for myself. But I also know that one of the fastest ways for me to improve my attitude is to find someone to connect with.

I love people, and I love hearing their stories. There's almost always something wonderful to be discovered about each human being I encounter. On this afternoon in Las Vegas, the wonderful human being was an older woman who came and sat in the chair opposite me.

I pulled myself out of my "poor me" attitude, smiled at her, and asked, "Where are you traveling to today, ma'am?"

"Flagstaff," she answered. "My grandson and I are going to the Grand Canyon. We've never seen it, and I've been saving a long time to get us there."

"Well, it's worth the trip—it's one of God's masterpieces," I told her. "How old is your grandson?"

> **When we connect, it doesn't just make us feel better; it makes us *do* better.**

"He's twelve," she said, and I noticed her eyes were a little misty. "I've got stage four leukemia, and I don't know how much longer I can travel. But I promised myself that I'd see the Grand Canyon before I die, and I want to give my grandson a memory he can treasure after I'm gone."

Just then a voice on the loudspeaker announced another delay on our flight. Amidst the groans of other travelers around us, this beautiful woman smiled and said, "I don't care if we have to wait all night for this flight. I've been waiting fifteen years to get there, and another hour or two sure won't matter to me!"

Before our respective flights were called, she and I chatted and laughed and shared our stories with each other. In that short time we made what I call a soul-deep connection. It was strong; it was positive; it was based on shared emotions. We both felt better for having spent time in each other's company. I felt uplifted and inspired and humbled by a woman who looked ordinary but who possessed an extraordinary beauty of spirit.

When we connect, it doesn't just make us feel better; it makes us *do* better. I have found that our success and fulfillment in life are closely tied to the quality of the connections we are able to create. When we connect to positive emotions, to great people, to companies and causes that make a difference, then we are more likely to achieve great things and feel great while doing so. But what this means is that we have to choose *who, what, why,* and *how* we will forge the connections in our lives. We have to make sure that the things we choose to put our passions into are worthy of us. We need our connections to pull us up rather than bring us down. And that's why I have devised a framework designed to help people CONNECT.

THE MEANING OF *CONNECT*

The word *connect* comes from two Latin words that mean "to bind or fasten together." But when it comes to building success in life, I have a specific definition of *connect* in mind:

CONNECT: To feel and/or create a strong, positive relationship with someone (an individual or group) or something (an idea, an institution, a cause, a mission, and so on). The ultimate result of this relationship should be uplifting both for the individual and for others.

When we talk about the power to connect, there are three key elements. First, to connect there must be an *emotional link*. Connecting is built around emotion. You can use your mind to connect with something or someone, but until you get your emotions involved, it's a weak connection at best. When you first join a company, you may or may not connect to the organization. But as you develop relationships with co-workers and feel that you are contributing to the company's mission, then you create an emotional link: you connect. You can feel connected to a team or a group of people; most of us feel connected to our family, for instance. You also can feel connected to an organization (a company, your church, your school, a fraternity or sorority, a volunteer group, and so on) or to an idea, mission, or concept.

Second, to connect we must create *a strong feeling*. Most of us don't feel especially connected with our casual acquaintances because we don't feel strongly about them. We do feel connected with really good friends because the emotions we experience in those relationships are a lot stronger. It's like the difference between watching a football game on TV for the entertainment value and cheering for your hometown team. Your feelings about the outcome of the game are a whole lot stronger because you're watching "your" team. It's also possible to connect with an idea, concept, or belief as long as we feel strongly about it. To connect, we take our belief in something and link it to our emotions. I feel strongly about my faith as a Christian. Patriotic individuals connect to the country where they live. You may connect strongly to your personal mission in life and your family.

The third part of the definition of *connect* is to create *a positive, uplifting relationship*. You can feel strongly about someone and hate that person's guts, but I wouldn't consider that a positive, uplifting relationship. I also wouldn't categorize gangs, or abusive relationships, or movements like fascism as positive or uplifting. Yes, all of these can create strong emotional links between people, but the results are terrible. I would not categorize these as the kind of connections most of us would seek.

Unfortunately, there are also some circumstances in business where people can create strong emotional links but the relationship is neither positive nor uplifting. Con artists are expert at creating strong emotional links, but with the goal of taking advantage of people. Some managers create strong emotional links through fear and intimidation and criticism. But do you feel connected to those managers in a positive, uplifting way? Of course not. That kind of emotion is destructive rather than constructive. It may produce results in the short term, but in the long run fear and intimidation lead to either depression or rebellion.

I believe that we are successful when we connect to an uplifting purpose in ways that produce positive, uplifting relationships. Great organizations foster the right kinds of connections between the company, its mission, and its employees. For example, over thirty-five years ago a little airline in the big state of Texas was struggling to succeed. The top management team came together with the goal of thinking outside the box, and what they created would transform not just the company and the lives of the people who would work there but also the airline industry itself.

The company was Southwest Airlines, and in the late 1970s

the management came up with two great ideas. First, they believed that they weren't competing for the customers of existing airlines. Instead, they wanted to attract the people who were driving and taking buses because airfare was too expensive. "We're in the mass transportation business," they declared.

The second great idea, however, has continued to make the biggest difference. Southwest connects to its employees first and its customers second. Management's goal was to create a fun, caring place to work—an airline that employees would be proud to work for, where their contributions would be recognized and rewarded. Southwest hires for attitude and trains for skills. They want people who like people, who believe in the Southwest approach and enjoy serving customers. The company's mission statement is "dedication to the highest quality of Customer Service delivered with a sense of warmth, friendliness, individual pride, and Company Spirit." In other words, connecting with customers while being connected to the spirit of Southwest.

The results of this drive to connect have been top-notch performance for over thirty years. Southwest was rated best airline for customer service six years in a row. They won the airline industry's "triple crown"—Best On-Time Record, Best Baggage Handling, and Fewest Customer Complaints—five years running. These awards are not possible unless employees of every stripe, from executives to flight attendants to gate agents to baggage handlers to cleaning crews, connect to the company and feel proud of their work. Not only that, the company has consistently returned a profit while many other airlines operate in the red. As my friend, mentor, and professional speaker former Southwest CEO Howard Putnam puts it, "Performance results when people believe and belong."

I believe in the kind of connections that inspire people to do their best and to feel their best doing it. I believe in connections that do good in the world and good for the folks who are investing their passion in life. Above all, I'm committed to showing you how the power to connect can help you do more, be more, feel more, and give more than you ever thought possible.

STRONG CONNECTIONS CREATE SUCCESS

When we truly connect with someone or something, we know it. When we connect with something or someone, our passion is engaged. When we feel connected, life is *goood!*

We can connect to something or someone in a moment. What's "love at first sight" if not connecting instantaneously with another person? Even if you haven't had that experience, most of us can remember a time when we connected instantly with someone at our first meeting. But to really connect—to build that emotional link and create a strong, positive, uplifting relationship—usually takes time. It takes our putting our emotions into the relationship and getting good feelings in return. When we build intense emotional links over a period of time, then our relationships can last forever.

Think about your favorite sports team. Why do you connect to them? Why do you celebrate when they win and feel down when they lose? Why do you follow their fortunes throughout the season? Why do you eagerly anticipate the first game and feel a little empty when the season's over no matter how well or ill your side fared? It's because you connect. When I was a kid my mom used to take me to the Garfield High School football games to watch Mark Williams, a good friend of the family, play. I still remember the band, the crowd, the excitement, and the joy we had cheering for *our* team. When our team won, we felt great. When they lost, we felt sad. But each week gave us another opportunity to cheer for our team. To this day I'll still call my buddy Calvin in Seattle and ask, "How's the Garfield football team doing?"

We see people all over the world who connect with their sports teams. We've all seen the rabid sports fans who wear the jerseys of the players on their hometown team, or paint their faces and their bare chests in the team colors and sit in subzero weather, risking pneumonia to display their team spirit. Recently I was talking with an older gentleman about football, and he told me he was an alumnus of Louisiana State University—LSU. The week before he had taken his grandson to an LSU game.

"Keith, if you ever get a chance to see LSU play football, make sure you get there at least two hours early and stand in the parking lot, by the door where the team enters the stadium," he told me. "The team gets off their bus about a mile away, and they parade into the stadium as a group. The parking lot is jammed with LSU fans cheering like mad for the team. Then the band follows the team into the stadium, and the fans cheer as loudly for the band as they did for the team!

"Right before the start of the game, the band marches from the end zone all the way across the field. I've been going to LSU games for over forty years, and in all that time I've never heard more than the first four notes of the LSU march—because after four notes the crowd goes crazy and you can't hear anything but cheering. If you want to see an entire stadium full of people connected to their team, watch the LSU Tigers. I'm in my late sixties, and I'm just like a kid when I go to those games."

We all want to be part of a team. We all want to win. We all want to connect intensely with something other than ourselves. What would happen if you deliberately used the power of connection to turbocharge every area of your life? Imagine the possibilities if you could capture the passion you feel toward your country's Olympic contenders or your favorite sports team and connect just as strongly to one another, to your job, to a goal! What incredible feats could you accomplish if you deliberately used your innate power of connection to fuel your performance? How much more success would you achieve? More important, how much more fulfillment would you feel at the end of the day knowing that you'd put not just your hands, not just your mind, but also your heart into your life?

ICARE

Caring is the key to connecting deeply. I know in some circles it's fashionable to appear blasé or even cynical about your job, your company—even your relationships. But caring makes the difference between a good relationship and an amazing one, and between a job you tolerate and one you can't wait to get to in the morning. You've got to care to connect, and real connection will increase your level of caring.

When you tap into your caring, you'll naturally seek ways to use that emotional link. Caring is like the electricity that runs through the wires of your house; it's the power that just waits until you plug something in. Just like electricity, though, the power of caring needs to be running through your heart and soul at all times. You don't wait until you need power for your computer to turn on the electricity in your house. In the same way, you need to "power up" your caring before you ever need it.

How do you keep the power of caring alive and flowing within you? I'm a big believer in affirmations—putting what we care about into words and declaring these truths out loud. I call these affirmations "ICARE" statements. Each statement begins with the words "I care," and the letters in ICARE stand for "Intensely Committed, Attentive, Ready, and Enthusiastic!" Here are some examples:

ICARE about myself.
ICARE about my life.
ICARE about my family.
ICARE about the fact that my family loves me.
ICARE about my success.

ICARE that I have a special gift.
ICARE that I'm empowered to make a difference for other people.
ICARE that I'm going to start taking better care of myself.
ICARE that I'm striving to do a better job.

What do *you* care about? Write your own ICARE list, and then repeat these ICARE statements daily. Even though you may not feel as if you care, you may not sense it, and you may not see it, you can start saying it. When you have a mind-set that says ICARE, over time you will change your beliefs. Your beliefs will change your attitude. Your attitude will help change your feelings. Your feelings will help change your actions. And your actions will help you to connect.

HOW TO CONNECT TO SUCCESS

Think of your life as a structure that you are building every day, room by room and floor by floor. The foundation of that structure is your attitude. A building is only as strong as its foundation, and a strong, positive, solid attitude will allow you to build a tall structure that will weather any storm.

The power to connect is the framework upon which you will construct the building for both personal and professional success. CONNECT is an acronym that represents your blueprint for creating powerful relationships and connections in every area. The seven steps represented by the seven letters in CONNECT contain principles to help you create the life and business you desire.

However, you can't just *do* something to connect; you also must *be* a certain way for those connections to work. Therefore, each step is accompanied by what I call a BE-Attitude. The BE-Attitudes provide a blueprint for becoming the best you can be. The seven CONNECT steps and BE-Attitudes will help you create success through people, purpose, and performance.

Here's a short description of each step and attitude.

CONNECT Step 1:
Commit to win

Before you ever take the shot or make the call or close the deal, you first have to commit to win. The most important commitment is with yourself: you must fully charge your internal "batteries" every single day so you'll have the energy and drive to do what must be done. Then you must lead the way for others by demonstrating the level of commitment required for outstanding performance.

The first BE-Attitude is to *be accountable*. Accountability is at the core of commitment. Without it, there is no loyalty and no lasting success. People and organizations are like sports teams: they can win only when the entire team is accountable and loyal. Start by being accountable, and you'll inspire others to be accountable as well.

CONNECT Step 2:
Open up to opportunities

Opportunities are all around us, but we must open our eyes and minds to see them. Opening up to opportunities means we must embrace diversity of thought, accept opinions different from our own, and overcome the biases we've adopted through our lives. We can use techniques like the Five-Second Opportunity Detector to get past our own mental limits and open up to the opportunities presented by and through others.

The second BE-Attitude is to *be a change embracer*. Change is the power for growth. If we don't change, we won't grow. To stamp out fear and embrace change, we must master the ability to listen and communicate. When we encourage dialogue and the open exchange of ideas, we create connections that lead to success.

CONNECT Step 3:
Notice what's needed and do what's necessary

Noticing what's needed and doing what's necessary means responding to the signals we get from others. We must do our best to supply respect and caring, two of the basic needs of every human being. We also must be proactive, taking action to create what people will call a "wow" experience because we are giving them what is necessary to create great results. We connect when we respect others enough to notice their needs, do what's necessary, and respond in a caring and positive way.

The third BE-Attitude is to *be aware.* We must recognize and focus on the needs of those around us. But to do so, we must learn to recognize our own value and build our self-esteem first. Then we can help others recognize their value and self-esteem as well.

CONNECT Step 4:
Navigate by your purpose

Each of us is born with a purpose and reason for living. We must discover our purpose and use it to navigate our way on this earth. When we discover our gifts and align our purpose with their expression, the world opens before us and our success is assured.

The fourth BE-Attitude is to *be vision centered.* Vision shows us what our purpose will look like as we go about living it every day. A life centered on vision will inspire us and keep us going through the tough times. With vision and purpose, we can accomplish great things.

CONNECT Step 5:
Execute ethically: Do what's right because it's right

Taking action is critical to accomplishing our vision, but all too often ethics are thrown overboard when things start to go wrong. Instead of asking questions like "Can we get away with this?" or "Will this make us the most money?" we must execute ethically and choose to do what's right because it's right.

The fifth BE-Attitude is to *be performance and integrity driven*. We cannot ignore either performance or integrity when it comes to our actions. We need to produce results, but to do so in an ethical manner. Only then will we achieve lasting success.

CONNECT Step 6:
Challenge your challenges

Everyone has challenges, but it's how we choose to meet them that will make the biggest difference. Instead of running from our challenges, we should run toward them. When we challenge our challenges and strive to overcome them, we connect with ourselves and with others at the deepest level.

The sixth BE-Attitude is to *be responsible*. Taking responsibility is the first step toward overcoming adversity. When we're responsible, we choose to respond rather than react to the professional and personal challenges that threaten to derail us. Instead of victims, we become victors on the battlefields of life.

CONNECT Step 7:
Transcend beyond your best

When we transcend, we go beyond challenging our challenges, even beyond the best we have been in the past, and we achieve a level of success that we never before thought possible. Organizations and individuals that reach and stay at the top always strive to go beyond their best. That's when life takes on new levels of significance and legacies are built.

The seventh BE-Attitude is to *be the difference.* If you've ever done something for other people to help them raise themselves up, you know how great it can feel. It connects you to yourself and your real purpose on earth like nothing else.

Here are the seven CONNECT steps and BE-Attitudes. You'll see how the first letter of each step spells out the word CONNECT.

THE 7 CONNECT STEPS AND BE-ATTITUDES

CONNECT Steps	BE-Attitudes
Commit to win.	**BE** accountable.
Open up to opportunities.	**BE** a change embracer.
Notice what's needed and do what's necessary.	**BE** aware.
Navigate by your purpose.	**BE** vision centered.
Execute ethically: Do what's right because it's right.	**BE** performance and integrity driven.
Challenge your challenges.	**BE** responsible.
Transcend beyond your best.	**BE** the difference.

The CONNECT steps are universal and inspirational. They are applicable whether you're building a sports team or a family, whether you're in a business or a church group, whether you're a

> **Connecting takes both action and attitude, both behavior and belief.**

CEO or an intern, whether you've been years in your position or it's your first day on the job. They will lead you to build the kind of strong, positive, uplifting connections with yourself, with other people, with your purpose and mission, and with your business or profession that can ensure you greater success and fulfillment in life.

While each step has great merit individually, they also build on one another. The rest of this book describes these steps, how they work, and how you can apply them in your life and business. You'll (1) identify behaviors that must change for you to put each principle into practice, (2) discover realistic ways to integrate the principle into your life and business, and (3) develop benchmarks to measure your results. Eventually CONNECT will become a way of life.

You are about to discover that connecting is not so elusive after all. It just takes the proper framework. Connecting takes both action and attitude, both behavior and belief. Within these pages lies your blueprint—so put on your hard hat and get to work.

CONNECT Step 1:
Commit to Win

They can because they think they can.
—*Virgil*

In 2000 the Baltimore Ravens football team was coming off a mediocre 8–8 season the year before. They hadn't even made the playoffs for their division. When the team reassembled for training camp that summer, the coach felt that the players had lost their confidence and their drive to win. They weren't acting like potential champions or believing that the new season could be different.

But the Ravens coach had other ideas. He brought in my great buddy Art Berg to speak to the team. Art had been a quadriplegic for seventeen years, ever since a car accident had robbed him of the ability to use his arms and legs. Yet Art traveled over 200,000 miles each year as an author and professional speaker.

Art inspired the Ravens players with his own story—but what turned the day was when he told them about an obscure English author, William Ernest Henley. Henley was afflicted with tuberculosis from an early age, and doctors in Scotland had had to amputate one of his legs below the knee because of it. They told Henley they would need to amputate the other foot to save his life. But Henley refused to let them do it. He kept his foot, battled back from the disease, and wrote a poem inspired by his struggle: "Invictus."

Invictus means "unconquered, unsubdued." You may remember some of the poem's verses:

> Out of the night that covers me,
> Black as the Pit from pole to pole,
> I thank whatever gods may be
> For my unconquerable soul.
>
> In the fell clutch of circumstance
> I have not winced nor cried aloud.
> Under the bludgeonings of chance
> My head is bloody, but unbowed.
> . . .
> It matters not how strait the gate,
> How charged with punishments the scroll,
> I am the master of my fate:
> I am the captain of my soul.

That year the Baltimore Ravens adopted "Invictus" as the slogan for their team. "Invictus" represented their determination to make their own fate no matter what the circumstances. It represented their commitment to win. The Ravens played like a different team that season, going all the way to the Super Bowl. Before the final game, the coach told them, "Whether we win or lose on that field today, we will play with the Invictus attitude. We will not be conquered no matter what the final score of the game." The Ravens were victorious, beating the New York Giants decisively.

The Baltimore Ravens CONNECTed to their goal of winning the Super Bowl. They were emotionally linked to the outcome, and they were willing to build the framework to support their success. While the foundation for CONNECT is a positive attitude, the first floor of the framework is to make the commitment to do whatever it takes to succeed. The first step of CONNECT is to *commit to win.*

> "The difference between success and failure is often about five percent more effort."
> —S. Truett Cathy

Among other definitions of *commit, Webster's New World Dictionary* gives this one: "to bind as by a promise; to pledge or engage." A commitment is dedication to a long-term course of action. When we decide to commit, we take a stand and declare that we are ready to put in the time, effort, and energy to get the job done no matter what. S. Truett Cathy is the founder and CEO of Chick-fil-A®, a chain of fast-food and stand-alone chicken restaurants throughout the United States. Mr. Cathy is a role model to me because he has built an incredibly successful business while adhering to the tenets of his faith. According to Mr. Cathy, the two key ingredients for success are hard work and commitment. "The difference between success and failure is often about five percent more effort," he has stated. "But we start to see miracles take place when we truly commit ourselves."

When we make the commitment, however, we also need to be clear about what "winning" will mean. Some people think winning means beating the other guy so soundly that he'll never get up again. Others think winning means you have to be better than anyone else. Sometimes it can seem that society defines winning as having the most money, the biggest house, or the most attractive husband or wife, or being the most famous person in your profession. But to truly commit to win, each of us must define winning for ourselves. My bookkeeper has a ninety-seven-year-old grandmother who gets out of bed every day with plans for what she wants to accomplish. She doesn't focus on the fact that she no longer can drive, has trouble walking, and has to rely on others to get groceries for her and help her with many tasks she used to do for herself. Instead, she wins when she accomplishes whatever her goals were for the day. And every night she goes to bed and thanks God for her blessings.

William Ernest Henley won when he kept his leg. Single moms all over the country win when they have enough food on the table for their kids. A fifteen-year-old in an urban neighborhood may win by turning down drugs. Your version of winning may include taking care of your family, doing a great job at work, living according to the principles of your faith, being a loyal citizen of your country. Winning simply means facing the tasks and challenges that life brings your way and committing to do your best and beyond your best in the battle. You have to decide to make winning a priority, and then commit your energy and focus to building the connection that will help you win. When you commit to win, you'll be astounded at the power that will flow through you as you bring all your resources to the fight. When you commit to win, you become the master of your fate and the captain of your soul.

MAKE A COMMITMENT TO YOURSELF

The most important commitment you can make is not with other people but with yourself. To accomplish your dreams and goals, you must fully charge your internal "batteries" every single day so you'll have the energy and drive to win. Each day before you leave the house, you need to do whatever it takes to create energy—physically, mentally, and spiritually. You have to plug into your own power source so you can charge through the day.

One of the best things you can do is to create your own "commit to win" routine that you use every single day to charge your internal batteries. What will you do when you wake up? Remember, this day was made for you to rejoice and be glad in.

Take a few moments to remind yourself that any day above ground is a great day. If you're above ground, you have another day to learn, to touch, to teach, and to make a mark on this world that cannot be erased.

Make a commitment to win by making the most of your day. Whom will you connect with? How will you touch their hearts and spirits? What gifts will you receive from them? What accomplishments will you achieve by working together? So many people tell me they have trouble being motivated. Well, to be motivated you need a motive, and love is the greatest motive of all. Remember, whatever you sow is what you will reap, so love your neighbor, your co-worker, and your teammate as you love yourself.

When you begin your day by committing to love yourself unconditionally, and committing to the source of all power, then each day will give you an opportunity to win. You'll find yourself ready to take on anything the day has to offer. More important, you'll develop the positive attitude that will carry you through the tough times and make others seek you out for your influence and inspiration. You'll find it's a lot easier to connect with others when you take those few moments to commit and connect with yourself.

COMMIT TO WIN MEANS YOU GO FIRST

In a lot of circles it's not "cool" to be seen as committed to something or even to someone. It's much cooler to be offhand, to pretend it's not a big deal, to play as if you can take it or leave it—whether it's a job or a relationship or an issue. And yet what are we always looking for from others? We want them to commit to us. We want the other guy to stick his hand out for the handshake. We want the other person to be the first to say, "I love you." We want our company to assure us that our jobs will be there for the long run before we put our hearts and souls into our efforts.

But what if it's *our* job to commit first? After all, the Golden Rule starts with *us* doing unto others the way we want them to do to us, not the other way round. To achieve success through people, purpose, and performance, we must be first to make a commitment. (In fact, to truly connect with others we need to follow what my friend and mentor Tony Alessandra calls the Platinum Rule: treat others the way they'd like to be treated, not the way you would like them to treat you.) Going first demonstrates that you are truly committed to win.

When you commit to win, you can be the spark that lights the fire of better relationships and superior performance. I read recently about Jaime Escalante, who taught at a high school in the barrio of East Los Angeles, where drugs and gangs are everywhere and the high school dropout rate averages over fifty percent. Mr. Escalante decided to prepare some of his students to take the advanced placement (AP) calculus test. Most of the kids he was teaching were barely passing math, and many didn't plan to finish high school. But Mr. Escalante committed to work with these kids and do whatever it took to get them ready for the test. He held sessions before school and on Saturdays. He worked with them individually to make sure they understood the math and were completely ready to succeed. The first year, two students passed the AP calculus exam. The next year it was seven students, and then fourteen. Within eight years, more students from Escalante's calculus program passed the AP exam than did the kids from prestigious Beverly Hills High.

Many of us have examples in our past of teachers, coaches, bosses, and mentors who committed to us long before we committed to them. They saw something in us that often we didn't even recognize in ourselves. But it wasn't just what they saw in us; what we remember is the fact that they committed their time, energy, and faith in who we were and what we could accomplish. I wouldn't be who I am today without the commitment of my mom, my grandmothers, and some of my teachers and speech therapists in grammar school. As a child I had a stuttering problem, and at times the other kids were merciless in making fun of me. However, my mom told me that she would get me the help I needed so that one day I'd be able to speak well. My speech therapist also was incredibly patient and kind. I felt that she was absolutely committed to helping me overcome my speech impediment. But just as important, I felt she connected to me as a person. I responded to this commitment and connection by working incredibly hard. And when I learned to speak clearly and slowly, it was a big victory for me and for all those who had committed to help me succeed.

If you are a manager, a boss, or an employer, committing to win and connecting are the two most important commandments you can follow. When employees or team members feel you are committed and connected to them, your workplace results will improve. People want to work for and with people who they feel support and appreciate them and who they believe are committed to helping them win.

Daniel Goleman, who wrote the book *Emotional Intelligence,* has been studying how people relate to one another—their "social intelligence." He asked groups from business, academia, non-profit associations, and social organizations all over the world to describe the qualities of a great boss. The responses were almost identical. "The best bosses are people who are trustworthy, empathic, and connected, who make us feel calm, appreciated, and inspired," Goleman reported. People view someone as a great boss when they feel connected and believe he or she has committed to helping them win. That level of commitment from a boss produces one of the most important yet undervalued qualities in the workplace today: loyalty.

> People view someone as a great boss when they feel connected and believe he or she has committed to helping them win.

ARE YOU LOYAL, OR "LOYAL UNTIL"?

A generation ago, people stayed at one company for their entire working lives. They worked thirty or forty years, collected their benefits, and retired. That's the way things were for our parents and grandparents. They gave the company their work and their loyalty, and they expected the company's loyalty in return.

Are things ever different today! Now companies are acquired or merge with one another or simply vanish at the drop of a hat. Jobs move overseas, and massive layoffs are common. All too often, people feel that the company's loyalty to them is only as good as the last paycheck they received—and there's no guarantee there will be another paycheck in the future.

However, this lack of loyalty cuts both ways. People entering the workforce today expect to work for seven to fifteen different companies over a lifetime. These individuals are valuable assets to a company while they are there. They will work hard to acquire skills that can carry them on to the next career opportunity. But they understand that their first commitment had better be to themselves.

It seems that most of us today live by a new definition: "loyal until." We are loyal until our significant other upsets us once too often. We're loyal until something or someone better comes along. In business, we're loyal until market conditions change, or a merger takes place, or the competition takes over. We're loyal until we feel threatened, and then we use that as an excuse to break faith with others. But I believe that this conditional commitment is like a cancer eating at the heart of our businesses and our relationships. If I feel I could be tossed out on my ear at any moment, why should I go the extra mile on my job? If I think my manager doesn't care about me as a person, why should I do anything to make him or her look good? Isn't it better just to put in the least amount of effort to get by?

I'm not saying that we need to go back to the good old days of lifetime employment. That's not realistic. Today's world of global competition and fast-moving business is not going to let us keep jobs just because we've been loyal employees. A company's commitment to us, or our commitment to a company, will change when conditions change. But I do believe that the secret to success and fulfillment at work is twofold. First, both you and the other party need to *be clear on the rules for the commitment.* And second, both parties need to *commit to create a winning relationship.* Only when workers and businesses commit to win will people put their whole hearts into their jobs.

1. Get clear on the rules

Most people don't want to do the same job forever. In fact, we want to move up in our professions, and often that involves going to another company. But it's critical that all parties involved know the rules of the game: the requirements of both employee and business to create a committed work relationship.

The rules of the game are designed to preserve the rights of both employers and employees. These rules should be communicated at the onset of an employment agreement or partnership. What are the expectations? What commitments are being made? If one party said he or she was going to perform A to Z but does only A to C, then the rules weren't followed as promised. In those circumstances, the other party has the right to be "loyal until." If, for example, someone goes to work for a company with the understanding that benefits will be paid, but those benefits are subsequently taken away, it is understandable that the employee will look for other options. If the employee is hired to do a particular job but is not performing up to standards, the company will either retrain the employee or let the employee go.

2. Commit to create a winning relationship

Some employers and bosses manage to gain loyalty from others in the midst of constant change. How do they do it? They follow the second requirement of professional success: they commit to create a winning relationship. Recently I was brought in to speak for a group of managers at Anthem Blue Cross and Blue Shield in Virginia. Anthem had just merged with Wellpoint, another huge health care provider, and a lot of changes were coming down the pike. The managers were so excited about my message on the importance of attitude that they booked me to speak to twelve hundred of their front-line associates—the people who actually enroll members and process claims. Not only did Anthem give people time off from work to attend my session, but they actually hired buses to bring associates from all over Virginia—a trip of two hours or more—because they wanted them to benefit from my message. These employees felt that the company was so committed to creating a winning relationship that it went the extra mile to promote their growth.

Anthem employees have responded to the company's commitment with dedication and loyalty. As Carla Y. Picard, Program Manager, Performance Support & Analysis, for Anthem Blue Cross and Blue Shield Virginia, told me recently, "Like much of corporate America, the health care industry has been through massive change over the past several years. After the Wellpoint merger, we were the nation's biggest provider of health care, and not too long ago we merged with another Blue Cross/Blue Shield corporation in New York. To say this has been a tumultuous time is an understatement. But we feel that the most important thing is for us to stay connected with one another, whether our boss or colleague is in the next office or a couple of states away. We're committed to keeping ourselves connected, focused and on the same page.

"Having speakers like Keith come in has given us a unifying

attitude. I talked to a manager in Virginia Beach today, and she told me she had played one of Keith's CDs in her team meeting that morning. We are all committed to keeping our team strong, supported, and with the right attitude, no matter how many changes our corporation goes through."

When we commit to win, we find that we are not fighting an uphill battle to gain agreement from others. Employers gain not just "buy-in" on a project, goal, or cause but true commitment from the people doing the work. Employees gain stability, a better work environment, and a sense of being on the same team. Commitment to win can uplift both performance *and* attitude. To me, that is a winning formula.

COMMITMENT IN CRISIS

Ed Doherty is a shining example of commitment in an industry not well known for employer or employee loyalty. Ed owned franchises for twenty-eight Roy Rogers restaurants in Connecticut, and all of them were making money. A few years later, Hardee's Food Systems bought the Roy Rogers chain from the Marriott Corporation. Some of the actions of the new owners sent Ed's business into a nosedive as both sales and profits declined. Ed had personally guaranteed the loans for his franchises, and one day he found that he owed the bank $4 million. To cover the loans he had to sell some of his restaurants to other chains. He convinced Wendy's to lend him money to convert six of his Roy Rogers restaurants to Wendy's. But Ed had to think about what to do with all the people who worked for him.

From the beginning Ed committed to do everything he could for his employees. He started by telling them the truth. He told them what he was doing and why it was necessary to sell certain restaurants and convert others to a different franchise. He told them, "When I sell a restaurant, you'll have the chance to go with it and keep your job. If I'm selling it to Taco Bell or McDonald's, I will not make the deal unless they agree to hire you at the same salary you're currently making. Obviously, it is your choice whether you want to work for them. But I will not let you be stranded without a salary." Ed also asked for commitment from his employees. "Because there is no future for you here, some of you will choose to leave before I am able to sell the restaurant where you work," he said. "If you do leave, please give me as much notice as possible, because I can't hire other people to come and do a job that's going to end."

In the restaurants Ed was keeping, he let the employees know up front there would be no raises or bonuses for a while. But he promised to keep them informed about the health of the business and to do everything in his power to turn things around.

The result? Virtually everybody stayed with Ed. The companies that bought his restaurants agreed to hire his managers at their same salaries. Ed handpicked those he wanted to run the six restaurants that were converted to Wendy's. Meantime, Ed was approved as an Applebee's franchisee. Three years later, he opened his first Applebee's; the following year he had three restaurants. Ed was making money again, so he went back to the employees who had been working in his Wendy's restaurants for three years without raises. Ed increased their salaries to make up for those years, paying them what they would be making had they gotten a raise each year.

Ed's people were loyal in the midst of extremely challenging changes because they felt he was committed to helping them win. They knew Ed to be a man of integrity, who would do what he said he would do. Ed's commitment created an environment of mutual respect, trust, and loyalty.

THE "COMMIT CONNECTION"

Employees today are not as motivated as they once were by authority or loyalty to a company. However, they *are* motivated when they feel respected, both as individuals and for their contribution. When that happens, they become loyal to the people for whom they work and, in turn, to the company. The unique corporate culture of DaVita Inc., the biggest provider of kidney dialysis services in the United States, produces that deep level of commitment.

Kent Thiry had created people-friendly environments in his previous CEO jobs, but when he became CEO of Total Renal Care he wanted to raise the bar. He wanted to create a community that would make Total Renal Care a truly special place to work. He started by involving employees in key decisions at the company. He wanted them to consider themselves not just employees but part of a community—a village. Even Thiry's title reflects his approach: the nameplate on his office door reads "Mayor of the Village."

When it came time to set out the company's core values, Thiry involved about eight hundred employees in the process. Employees deliberated for eight months and voted to adopt six core values: Service Excellence, Integrity, Team, Continuous Improvement, Accountability, and Fulfillment. A seventh value, Fun, was added later.

As the policies, practices, and spirit of the company evolved, many employees wanted to change the company name because they felt "Total Renal Care" no longer represented their values and mission. Here, too, Thiry asked employees for their input. The name chosen was *DaVita,* which in Italian means "He or she gives life." That type of employer-encouraged citizen involvement is what inspires the employees to live out the mission and values of the DaVita "Village." For a company that services approximately 1,255 outpatient dialysis centers in 41 states and

the District of Columbia, creating a village-like atmosphere is a
true labor of love on the part of employees and management
alike.

A COMMITMENT TO RECOGNIZING
AND REWARDING EXCELLENCE

DaVita continues to recognize and reward the commitment of
its employee citizens. Every year, the company's management
chooses as many as one hundred fifty citizens as Shining Stars.
These nurses, technicians, and other employees go the extra mile
with patients, giving them holiday gifts or comforting family
members. They work overtime when a teammate is sick, or provide extra training or emotional support to a teammate who is
trying to learn how to administer dialysis. They are role models
of the company's mission and values. DaVita honors these
Shining Stars at the company's annual management meetings.

DaVita is dedicated to the constant growth of its employees.
The DaVita Academy was formed to bring together nurses, technicians, administrative assistants, accounts payable clerks, and all
frontline teammates for personal growth and to learn more
about the DaVita Village. The Academy philosophy is that if you
are going to become a DaVita citizen, you should understand the
history and development of the Village and what it stands for.
The sessions have nothing to do with teaching teammates how to
be more productive in carrying out specific job duties. Instead,
they focus on the company's mission and values.

Another example of village mentality is the DaVita Village
Network, an employee-to-employee safety net to help teammates in the event of a personal crisis. "If you live in a village and
someone gets hurt or their spouse gets cancer or their car burns
up, you would help them," Thiry said recently. "You would baby-
sit for their kids while they go to the hospital. If they didn't have

a car, you would leave your house early to pick them up and take them to work. We wanted to be that kind of village." The company matches every dollar a teammate contributes to the DaVita Village Network. When tragedy strikes, money is available to pay for extra day care, allow a person take off work and still draw a salary, or pay for medical bills and drug costs that are not covered by an insurance plan. More than 1,200 teammates have voluntarily had money deducted from their paychecks for the DaVita Village Network fund, which has paid out more than half a million dollars to more than one hundred families.

Do you think DaVita employees are loyal? You bet—because they feel that they are citizens of a community that cares. They're committed to one another, to the company, and to its mission and values. As a result of this commitment, contributions to the DaVita Village Network fund continue to rise. DaVita has the best clinical outcomes in its industry. In just six years the company saw its stock price skyrocket and employee turnover cut in half.

This past summer I got a call from DaVita: they wanted to fly to my home in Florida so I could videotape a message for their employees. "We have 29,000 team members, and over 12,000 of them are celebrating their fifth anniversary with our company," they told me. "We want you to congratulate them and tell them you look forward to celebrating their tenth anniversary with the company." It was an honor for me to tape that message for a company that I believe is a shining example of committing to win.

THE "PERKS" OF COMMITMENT

Most people get up and go to work in the morning to bring home a paycheck to take care of their families. But when we truly commit, the quality of our lives is increased by far more than monetary gain. We create a sense of *belonging* when we partner with others to rally around a common goal. We experience the *pride of achievement* that boosts our self-esteem. We gain *skills* that can propel us forward, opening up new professional and personal opportunities. And, according to my "mental toughness" coach, Steve Siebold, when we realize the personal benefit of our commitment, we leave middle-class performance and *become world-class performers.*

When you are a world-class performer, you can work anywhere you want. You can even start your own business. A company might benefit from an employee's commitment for the short term, but the personal benefit of world-class commitment can last a lifetime.

Seeing the potential for personal benefit motivates people. So does working for a purpose beyond yourself. Your motivation to commit depends on the answer to one very important question: Why are you going to work each day? If the reason behind your work is meaningful, then passion for your job comes easily. After all the hard work, blood, sweat, and tears, will you be able to look back and say you made a difference? Will you be able to look back with pride? Will you have done something that matters, something to better the lives of others? When your work has meaning beyond personal gain, your commitment level and resulting success will soar.

CARE FOR YOUR PEOPLE AND THEY'LL CARE ABOUT THE JOB

As vice president and "chief people officer" of the Maggiano's Little Italy and co-founder of the Go Roma Italian Kitchen restaurant chains, Yorgo Koutsogiorgas is truly committed to his employees, which explains why retention is off the charts at virtually every one of his eateries. In the restaurant business, sixty to one hundred percent turnover is commonplace. Restaurant owners that have only fifty percent employee turnover are considered geniuses. During Yorgo's tenure, overall yearly turnover at the twenty-eight Maggiano's restaurants was an amazing *ten percent*. And after being in business for two years, his Go Roma restaurants had absolutely no management turnover.

Why? Yorgo's personal philosophy is centered on building relationships. "Far too many companies don't see beyond the transaction," he says. "They see employees and customers for what they can do for the company, but don't care about the employees and customers on a personal level." Yorgo knows the names of the spouses and children of every dishwasher, server, and manager. He asks how the employees are, and whether their kids played Little League over the summer. People who have worked with Yorgo stay in touch with him years after they have left the restaurant because they know he truly cares for them.

Yorgo believes you must prove to people that you are committed to them *before* you ask them to be there for you. And he lives it. He is always on the front line with his employees. When they see him on his knees picking up trash from under a table, they don't think twice about doing it themselves.

Because employees know Yorgo cares, they feel comfortable enough to tell him when they are going through personal challenges. They also know their employer will go the extra mile for them. When one employee told Yorgo that he had failed to sign up for health insurance and now his wife needed a hysterectomy, Yorgo first expressed empathy and concern, and then he extended the employee a short-term, no-interest loan to help with the immediate crisis.

Another employee had full health coverage, but the insurance

> **You must prove to people that you are committed to them *before* you ask them to be there for you.**

company denied claims for her son's severe hearing impairment because the condition was considered to be preexisting. The woman's plight became Yorgo's personal crusade. He took a crash course in legal matters involving insurance. He learned all about what constitutes a preexisting condition. Then he called decision makers at the highest level of the insurance company and appealed to their compassion and logic. The result? The insurance company reversed its decision and covered the son's treatment. The employee and her family have moved to another state, but she still calls occasionally and also sends Yorgo Christmas cards.

Yorgo invests in people, and his return is both personally and monetarily rewarding. As a result, his restaurant ventures have enjoyed amazing success. Less than two years after Yorgo founded the Go Roma Italian Kitchen chain, he had restaurants in four locations and contracts for three more in the Chicago metro area. Expansion plans are in the works to build Go Roma restaurants in the San Francisco Bay area and Los Angeles. And Yorgo is still aiming for employee retention of ninety percent or more in each restaurant in the chain.

CARE + RESPECT = RETENTION

Whether someone is delivering the company mail or making decisions on million-dollar acquisitions, he or she is looking for the same two things: care and respect. To retain employees, managers must commit to make an employee who has been doing the same job for seven years feel just as valuable as the person who is rapidly promoted through the company ranks. When people feel that their managers and co-workers care about them and respect them, they will return the favor by working hard and staying committed.

The Virginia call center for Anthem Blue Cross and Blue

Shield has broken the record for retention in its industry, with several service employees boasting double-digit tenure—unusual in a call center environment. Anthem's call center has so many longtime employees that a special club has been established to recognize those who have worked there for more than twenty years. One woman recently retired after forty-six years with the company.

Why do Anthem employees stay for so long? Program Manager Carla Picard says that it's because they know the company cares about them and is committed to helping them be their best. Call center personnel constantly hear directly from executive management about the importance of their service role to the organization and to the corporate strategy. Treating members with care and respect comes easily for Anthem call center employees because they receive care and respect from high-level Anthem executives.

Anthem demonstrates its commitment to all of its employees in hundreds of ways. Each year the company selects a small number of its associates as Service Heroes—people who represent the level of service Anthem strives to fulfill every day. These Service Heroes are acknowledged at an annual company-wide banquet held in Richmond, Virginia. They stay in the city's finest hotel, they're chauffeured to the banquet in stretch limos, and during the evening they're given trophies and acknowledged with a special video presentation.

Anthem's commitment to its employees includes taking care of them in good times and bad. For example, instead of immediately laying off staff when particular roles are no longer needed, Anthem creates a resource team to determine whether there is another place in the company for those employees. If not, the resource team helps employees polish their resumes and then brings in outside consultants to assist employees with their job searches. To me, this shows that Anthem's care and respect are more than a means of retaining employees. They're a reflection of the commitment to win that is the hallmark of a world-class organization.

One of my great mentors, Bob Moawad, reminded me, "People don't care how much you know until they know how much you care about them." Bob Moawad was a living example of the power of caring. I first took Bob's course, "Increasing Human Effectiveness," as I was experiencing challenges at IBM. I learned from Bob to use affirmations, and he reminded me of the importance of setting goals. Through his tapes and learning systems, Bob mentored me through my early years of speaking on attitude. We reconnected a few years ago because I wanted him to know the impact he had on my life and that I was now a motivational speaker.

Bob was a living example of the power of attitude. Diagnosed with cancer, he lived eight years beyond the life expectancy the doctors gave him. Even when he was sick, tired, and weary, whenever anyone asked Bob how he was, he'd say, "I'm great!" He cared for his family, his business associates, and thousands of people like me whom he taught and mentored over the years.

When your team members feel your commitment to them as people, when they know you care for and about them, when they sense you're committed not just to the work they can produce for you but also to their growth, success, and happiness, then you'll be on the way to building a team that can accomplish miracles. Like the Super Dogs of Garfield High, you'll be ready to win it all. And what a celebration that will be!

ACCOUNTABILITY:
THE BUILDING BLOCK OF TRUST

The only way to build commitment is through trust, and trust is built with accountability. Therefore, the BE-Attitude of the first

CONNECT step is to *be accountable.* We must keep our promises to ourselves and to others. We must be willing to be judged not by our good intentions but instead by our concrete results.

A few years ago I was to be the closing speaker for a national sales conference for Kodak. I was really looking forward to the opportunity, and I was excited about sharing my message with this group of super-motivated performers. Now, usually I arrive quite early for any speech, but that day there was a traffic accident on my route. I walked into the hotel at about 8:05 AM—plenty of time to go on at 8:30, according to schedule, or so I thought.

But when I asked the front desk clerk where the Kodak meeting was, she told me (very pleasantly) that there was no Kodak meeting scheduled that day. It's a good thing I'm committed to having a great attitude no matter what, because otherwise I would not have been in a great state when I heard that! I called my office and discovered that I was in the right hotel chain, but the wrong hotel. The Kodak meeting was all the way across town, forty minutes away. I looked at my watch: it was 8:10 AM. I was due onstage in exactly twenty minutes.

When I say I'm going to do something, I hold myself accountable for the commitment, even if it means doing what seems impossible. "Call Kodak and tell them I'm on my way!" I yelled into my phone at my office manager as I sprinted out of the lobby and back to the parking lot. I jumped into my rental car and peeled out of the lot. I broke every speed limit and drove like a maniac, praying the entire time that I could make it in time safely and without the police throwing me in jail. I walked onto the stage at Kodak at 8:29 AM, out of breath but honoring my commitment to my audience and myself.

Commitment to win requires us to be accountable. If we're not accountable, any commitment we make is nothing but a promise written in water, and any connection is lost due to lack of trust. But how many times have you been affected by someone's lack of accountability? The supplier that swears "It'll be there by Thursday," yet on Monday you're still waiting; or the boss that promises to finish your performance review "next week," and yet somehow it's a month later and you haven't been able to meet with her. And when in your own life have you failed to keep your word about the big or the little things? Every broken promise is another chip in the foundation of our ability to commit to win. Every time we fail to be accountable, we are shaking our own certainty as well as the certainty others have about our trustworthiness and commitment.

There are several reasons for a lack of accountability: (1) fear, which often keeps us from taking responsibility and doing what we need to do; (2) excuses for our failure: we didn't have enough money to spend, or enough training, or we ran out of time; or (3) blame: it was someone else's fault. Instead of being accountable, too many companies have become a haven for finger-pointers. Funny thing about finger-pointing, though: when one finger points out, the other three are pointed right back at ourselves. To be truly accountable, you must eliminate the blame, excuses, and fear that bind you, and take ownership of your actions.

HOW'S YOUR ACCOUNTABILITY SCORECARD?

Personal accountability is critical to fostering the connections that build success. Before you can look outward and have a meaningful connection with others, however, you must look inward. *You are made in the image of greatness, and all things are possible to those who believe.* Accountability begins with belief in yourself and your abilities. Once you believe in yourself, you must then be accountable to take the actions necessary to turn your dreams into action and results. You must value yourself and the importance of keeping your word. Once you understand your value, you can start to build self-respect, and self-respect will not allow you to disappoint others or yourself. That's when accountability will become second nature.

One way to be accountable is to keep an *accountability scorecard.* In school, we had report cards to measure our efforts and performance. Today most businesses and organizations also measure performance. Companies have learned that a great return on assets (ROA) will come only when there is an equivalent ROA— Return On Accountability. It is only when the individuals in an organization are accountable that the organization as a whole will see an increase in profitability, market share, and bottom-line success.

To move forward as an individual, you must measure your performance. Are you accountable to yourself? Are you honest with yourself, or have you fooled yourself into thinking that you're okay when you're not? Have you lowered your personal standards of excellence? You may know, for example, that to be healthy you need to get up early and work out. Are you up at five o'clock, or are you hitting that snooze button when the alarm goes off each morning? Maybe you need to eat more nutritious meals and less junk food. What's your score in that area? How many fast food wrappers would we find in your car? You may feel that you need to read an inspirational or educational book each month. Have you done it? You want to read that book, but it's so much easier to sit on the couch with the remote in your hand.

There are things you need to do to take care of yourself and to accomplish your goals. Are you doing them? Score what you did yesterday, measuring internally and externally. How accountable are you to yourself? Are you taking the necessary actions to accomplish any of your goals? If not, what changes do you need to make now to improve for tomorrow?

Accountability means taking a stand and doing whatever it takes to honor your commitments. You will struggle to be accountable to others if you aren't accountable to yourself. If you're going to "sleep in" on you, you will more than likely sleep in on others. If you aren't doing what you need to take care of your personal responsibilities, how much discipline will you have to fulfill your responsibilities to others? Score your accountability to yourself, make the necessary changes for growth, and you will naturally score higher in your accountability to others.

Whether it's with your job, your team, your friends, or your family, when you are committed to winning together you will be accountable for doing whatever it takes to make that happen. You won't leave when things get tough. Instead, you will work through the hard times. Do you need to make some personal changes so your family or team can win? If you are committed, you will be accountable for making those changes. Do you need to grow your skills to reach your company's goals? Then you will be accountable for taking courses or acquiring the necessary skills. Does the company need you to put in some unpaid overtime? If you feel the company is committed to you, and you understand the big picture and the potential long-term personal benefit—that is, if you are focused on the end result—you'll be accountable for putting in the time, the talent, and the tenacity needed for success.

ACCOUNTABILITY AS MOTIVATION

Being held accountable for our results is one of the surest paths for growth in this world. We may not like deadlines, sales quotas, or performance reviews, but they certainly are a great motivator for getting us up off our butts at times!

Imagine an athlete who wants to be a world-class runner. He's out there every day, running his heart out, doing his best, and getting better all the time. But unless he uses a stopwatch to time himself, how's he going to know whether he's running faster or slower over the same distance? If he doesn't race against other athletes, how will he know whether he's doing well compared with people who are at the top of their game? If your goal is to be world class, then being accountable to achieve certain results is the only way to get there.

We live in a results-oriented world, with increasing pressure on the bottom line. That's why accountability is so critical in business as well as in life. Without accountability to standards, performance, and measurements, individuals ultimately fall into complacency, or what I call a rut. And the only difference between a rut and a grave is the dimensions.

I said earlier that commitment requires everyone to know the rules of the game and agree to them. Well, being accountable means that you must not only know the rules but also play by them. You can't get an exemption because you're a nice guy, nor can you follow only the rules you like and agree with. Once the rules are defined, you must be accountable for following them to the best of your ability.

When I was playing basketball, there were times when I believed that the referee had made a bad call—he thought I had fouled someone when I didn't, or I was sure I had been dribbling the ball when he called me for traveling. I quickly discovered that arguing with the referee was a waste of time, breath, and energy. The ref knew the rules and so did I, but he wore the black-and-white striped shirt and got to make the final call. I realized that the referee's call almost always stands, so I might as well get used to it.

The same thing is true in life. There are certain people and standards we agree to be accountable to. In a marriage, you vow to be faithful. In your work, you agree to produce certain results. If we don't meet those standards, you can expect to be called on it. And no matter how much you may not like the call sometimes, you have to be willing to play by the rules and let others make the calls that you follow.

MAKE SURE YOU'RE ASKING
FOR THE RIGHT RESULTS

It's great to hold yourself and other people accountable, but you'd better be sure you're holding them accountable for the right results and to the right standards. Otherwise, you'll see commitment dwindle and die. That's exactly what happened in a certain call center. The call center was told that its goal was to "increase productivity." The customer service representatives in the group were held accountable for reducing the amount of time customers were kept on hold. But that meant customer service reps felt pressured to rush calls when the customer got on the line. The time on calls was shorter, but the employees felt that all the education and product knowledge they had was now invalid and useless. They were disgruntled and had no feeling of loyalty. And because customers felt rushed, the competition was able to lure them away—all because the employees were being held accountable for the wrong results and the wrong standards.

There's a better way to achieve results, and that's to make sure that what you're accountable for will produce the results you want. In this case, why was the goal of "increased productivity" defined as shorter hold time for customers? Wouldn't it be better to use "customer satisfaction" and "increased customer purchase" as standards for increased productivity of a service department like a call center?

One of the keys to achieving the kind of accountability that produces world-class results is the willingness on both sides—employee and employer—to look with a fresh and unbiased eye at how those results are best achieved. That may mean changes in accountabilities, strategies, benchmarks, and procedures. But how much more will be achieved when all participants are confident that the actions they're taking are going to produce the world-class results they desire?

In the case of the call center, what if employees had been accountable for answering all the customers' questions while they were on the phone? That might have meant adding more customer service reps, or perhaps cross-training people from other departments and calling on them during busy times. Instead of saying, "Spend less time on the phone with each customer," the company could have said, "When the customer gets on the line, spend the time to answer all their questions." Eventually the number of times customers needed to call in would decrease, easing the work load and accomplishing the original goal to shorten customer hold times.

Companies need to remember that while results are important, the people who get those results are the company's biggest resource. Therefore, companies need to be accountable to their people so their people will be accountable for the results. Smart companies today are people centric; they put their people first because they know that committed and connected people will be accountable for world-class results.

MEASURING YOUR ACCOUNTABILITY AT WORK

One of the most common tools in business for promoting accountability is the performance appraisal. Most people approach their performance appraisals with some excitement and some fear. After all, nobody likes the feeling of being judged by others. But a great performance appraisal is really nothing but an accountability scorecard for your employer as well as for you.

In my first year at IBM, I had a super manager, Cobey Sillers, who was an ex-Marine and a great mentor. I hadn't taken any business courses in college, so there was a lot I didn't know. Cobey had taught me how to document my calls, how to write a good proposal, and how to explain and sell that proposal to clients. I had learned a ton from Cobey through the year, and I had produced some great results. I'd won a marketing award, and I'd made the IBM 100 Percent Club. (The 100 Percent Club was the ultimate goal of every IBM salesperson. To join, you had to make 100 percent of your yearly sales quota, and those goals always were very high—at least, I felt mine were.)

So when it came time for my performance appraisal I was feeling pretty good. Now, at IBM you're rated between a 1 and a 5. You get a 1 when you walk on water. A 3 is considered satisfactory. If you get a 5, you know to start looking for another job. I walked into Cobey's office expecting either a 2 or a 3.

Cobey took me through everything I'd committed to do in the previous year. "Keith, you did a great job in a lot of ways, but you missed some of your goals," he said. "And I notice that the company gave you some relief [meaning extra help]."

"The entire division was given some relief," I reminded him.

"That's true, and we're here to talk about you," Cobey said. "Based on the goals you set for yourself and the results you attained this year, I'm going to give you a rating of 4."

Only a 4? I was shocked. A performance rating of 4 meant no raise for a long time, and I'd need to hit a lot more benchmarks over the next year to raise my rating. But then Cobey explained to me exactly why he was giving me a 4. He laid out all the areas in which I could improve in the coming year. He helped me create a plan to increase my skills and performance, and together we set up benchmarks so we would both know I was holding myself accountable for creating the kind of results the company wanted.

I walked out of that office excited. "I got a 4!" I proclaimed proudly to the guy sitting in Cobey's outer office. "I understand exactly why I deserved it! And I'm never gonna get a 4 again!" And for the next twelve years at IBM, you'd better believe I never received a 4 rating again.

Performance appraisals help create commitment and accountability for employees and managers. When they're done well, they can be a way of connecting—something to be anticipated rather than dreaded. Twice a year, Yorgo Koutsogiorgas sits down with each of the employees of his restaurants, from dishwashers to managers, for formal appraisals. He reviews their performance, praises them for their positive accomplishments, encourages them to work through difficulties, and challenges them to pursue opportunities that will take their performance to the next level. Together they collaborate on creating action steps to make improvements where necessary. Six months later, Yorgo follows up to determine whether the employee had carried out the agreed-upon action plan.

Yorgo puts everything in writing—accolades as well as the details of the action plan—giving employees tangible accountabilities. In truth, however, what employees really remember is the fact that their boss values them enough to take thirty minutes to sit down with each of them and talk about how they can grow in their jobs. During one performance appraisal, Yorgo addressed the shortcomings of an employee I'll call Sam. What started as a discussion about tardiness and dependability led to Sam's confession of his struggle with substance abuse. Promising confidentiality, Yorgo paid for and helped Sam enroll in a substance abuse program. Yorgo also agreed to pay for three therapy sessions so that Sam could try to get at the root of his problem. Sam accepted Yorgo's help and today is drug and alcohol free, living a productive and successful life.

Sam was held accountable to timeliness and dependability. But how much more was accomplished because Yorgo approached accountability with sincere interest and care about Sam as a person, not just as an employee? How much more did I learn from Cobey Sillers at IBM because I felt that he cared for me and wanted me to be my best? I believe every employer and employee can learn from the examples of these great managers. When we measure not only by the numbers but also by the heart, we get increased commitment to accountability that takes results to the next level.

ACCOUNTABILITY SAYS ICARE

If you are leading people, accountability starts with you. You have to be the one who sets the bar by being accountable yourself, and then by holding others to a high standard of accountability. But leaders create accountability in two ways: through fear, or through connection. I think we've all seen (or worked for) leaders who tried to drive people to do their jobs by threatening them. That kind of leadership by intimidation never works in the long run. But if the people you're leading feel you truly care about them, that you're committed to helping them do a great job while holding them to the same high standards you set for yourself, then you'll find that your team will walk through walls and achieve the seemingly impossible. They'll be more likely to hold themselves accountable rather than expect you to do it for them. As long as they feel you're committed to them, they'll be committed to you.

However, as a leader you shouldn't assume you have your team's commitment right from the start. Loyalty is built over time. It's not an overnight process or a "microwave" approach. It doesn't happen instantly. Especially if you're a new manager, you're going to be tested. You'll have to deal with any "attitude baggage" your team may be carrying from previous leaders. You'll have to prove to your team that you're accountable and committed to them.

Several years ago I interviewed Mel Blount, a truly inspirational mentor. Mel played football for the Pittsburgh Steelers for many years, and when he retired he started a youth camp for kids in trouble. Mel knows about having to prove commitment and accountability to a very doubting "team" of kids. Mel and his counselors build trust slowly. Right from the start, they hold the kids accountable for basic things, like being punctual and doing certain chores. But they also make sure the counselors are available to the kids 24/7 for comfort, guidance, and direction. As the kids learn that the counselors truly care about them and are committed to their welfare, they start to open up and trust. And with trust comes a willingness and a desire to do more and be accountable for themselves. Mel has hundreds of kids who are a testament to Mel's heart and his dedication—his commitment to win.

Leaders go first. Leaders are accountable. Above all, leaders are committed to helping those they lead to win. To succeed, you must always be accountable for your team. It's the first, and most important, commitment you will make—because it makes all success possible.

COMMIT TO WIN ACTION STEPS

1. Where are you committed to winning? What commitments are you ready to make at work, at home, and with friends and family? Write the statement "I'm committed to win in the following areas . . ." and then make a list of all the key areas of your life.

2. Now focus on the greater purpose behind committing to win. Why are these areas important to you? What people will be affected by your commitment to win? How will your commitment uplift them? How will these commitments enrich your life? What is your greater purpose?

3. How are you going to commit to win with yourself? What routines will you put in place? How energized will you feel when you take a few minutes to welcome the day and connect to your source of power?

4. What does your business, company, or organization expect of you, and what do you expect of it? Are your expectations unreasonable? Do you feel that the company's expectations of you are unreasonable, too? You may need to sit down with your supervisor and/or employees and make sure both sides agree on the rules of the game. Once you've reached consensus, it will be easier to commit to a winning relationship.

5. What commitments are you determined to keep even when things are difficult? Remember Ed Doherty, who had to reduce his employees' salaries and eliminate bonuses when his business downsized, but who restored their lost wages when he was on his feet again. What examples do you have in your own life of keeping commitments in hard times?

6. How are you creating a "village" in your company? Even if your boss isn't as warm or forthcoming as Kent Thiry, you can start building strong connections with co-workers yourself. The greater the connections in your workplace, the more supported your team will feel, and the better results you're likely to achieve.

7. How are you recognizing and rewarding excellence? Acknowledging others is one of the best ways to create commitment. Again, don't feel you have to wait for upper management or your bosses to recognize outstanding performance. What if you gave out a monthly award to the best team member, or the person who went the extra mile to cover for someone who was sick, or the person who made the workplace fun? And remember, awards and recognition should flow up, down, and sideways. If your boss or supervisor deserves recognition, give it to him or her. Everyone loves a well-deserved pat on the back!

8. How are you showing your co-workers, employees, and bosses the level of care and respect that will encourage them to commit to your business or team? Have you experienced problems with employee retention? You might want to contact employees who have left to find out their reasons for leaving. If the reasons are emotional, what can you do to create a more supportive work environment?

9. How are you being accountable to yourself? You can't be accountable to others until you're accountable in your personal life. What's one area in which you need to increase your commitment to accountability? How will you show yourself and others that you're now accountable for greater results in your life?

10. Who's the umpire in your game of life? Who's setting the rules for accountability? Remember, you can argue with the referee until you're blue in the face, but it rarely does any good, and sometimes you get thrown out of the game. Figure out the rules, and then decide how you will follow them.

11. What's your accountability scorecard at work? What are you accountable for? What are you not accountable for? Do you and your employees/employer agree on your accountability? Perhaps, like Yorgo Koutsogiorgas, you need to do performance appraisals for your team or to request one from your manager. What action plan will you create to help you increase your accountability scorecard?

12. What ICARE statements will you add to your list to help you remember to commit to connect and be accountable?

13. Fill in the blanks: **ICARE to take action now by doing**

_____

to commit to win for _____

(my team, key people, etc.).

CONNECT Step 2:
Open Up to Opportunities

It's a funny thing about life: if you refuse to accept
anything but the best, you very often get it.
—*W. Somerset Maugham*

In the early 1970s Herman Boone became head football coach of the T.C. Williams High School in Alexandria, Virginia. Boone, an African-American, was selected over the popular white coach, Bill Yoast. That year, as part of a plan to integrate its schools, the city of Alexandria reshuffled its three high schools and sent all juniors and seniors to T.C. Williams. As a result, the football teams for one black school and two white schools were combined into one team. But at that time the white and black players had no interest in working with one another, not even with the goal of a winning football season. The other white assistant coaches weren't thrilled about a black head coach, either.

However, Boone believed that combining white and black players on one team meant enormous opportunity. He drilled the players together day in and day out. Eventually, the players realized they had something in common: they all were fiercely determined to win. As they opened to the opportunities represented by their new team, they formed a strong, cohesive unit. The T.C.

Williams Titans had an undefeated season and went on to win the state high school football championship. What's more, as the football team won game after game, the community found itself pulling together as well. People reached across their prejudices to support the players, both black and white.

To build bridges across barriers requires the second CONNECT principle: *open up to opportunities.* Life is constantly presenting us with opportunities. Every moment something new, wonderful, and exciting awaits us. Around the next corner may be the most important customer of your career. At the other end of the phone may be the love of your life or the perfect job offer. The next book you read may give you an idea or a new way of looking at things that will completely transform your life. The next obstacle you face may help you grow far beyond anything you ever felt was possible and achieve new levels of success.

But for any of this to occur, you must open up to the opportunities that come your way. And that requires you to do something that most people find extraordinarily difficult: embrace change. The BE-Attitude for this step is to *be a change embracer.* Most of the time, change is coming whether we want it to or not—so doesn't it make sense to be on the same side? When you embrace change you will find that you open up to opportunities that will help you CONNECT to yourself, your purpose, and your team.

DON'T LET YOURSELF STAGNATE

Think about water in a backyard pond. When you first put water in a pond, it's healthy and vibrant. It'll support fish and plant life. But if you keep the same old water in the pond week after week, pretty soon it gets stagnant. The fish and plant life in the pond become poisoned with waste and eventually die. For the pond to support life, you have to recirculate the water or, better yet, add new water frequently. When you do that, the fish and plants will thrive for a long time.

Like a pond, each of us has a certain amount of mental, emotional, and physical "water"—meaning our thoughts, our actions, our history, and so on—at any given time. That water does a pretty good job of supporting our lives at their current levels. But unless we add fresh water all the time in the form of new experiences, new ways of thinking, new beliefs, and new ideas, then we too become stagnant.

The last time you were faced with a new idea or a different way of looking at something, how difficult did you find it to open up to opportunities? All too often we get stuck in our prejudices and old ideas because we feel they're right. We don't even see opportunities until we're forced to do so. Closing yourself to opportunities keeps you stagnant, and in today's accelerated world of life and business, stagnant means failure. Stagnant means left behind. Stagnant means never growing or learning, as we were born to do.

Just think about the changes that have occurred in the past ten to twenty years. The Internet. Cell phones. Podcasts. Instant messages. Today you can be halfway around the world from loved ones and/or business associates and see them through videocast and hear them via satellite phone. New drugs and treatments can cure diseases once thought incurable. You can be in your company headquarters in the United States, go on a computer and change manufacturing specifications for a product in a factory in China, and the machine in China automatically will implement the change.

Now imagine what would happen if you closed your mind to all these opportunities. You'd still be using a rotary telephone and doing business by fax and snail mail. It would take days or weeks to make changes in your company's products. You might not benefit from the latest medical treatments because you weren't interested in any "newfangled" medicine.

In the same way you need to open up to the opportunities represented by the technological innovations that surround you constantly, it's even more important that you open up to the people and ideas you encounter on a daily basis. We have to open ourselves up to the opportunities that life constantly presents to us and embrace the changes that come our way. If we do so, then we find ourselves growing—almost without having to think about it.

ARE YOU A CHANGE RESISTER OR A CHANGE EMBRACER?

Opening up to opportunities isn't always easy, especially when it involves change. For some people change is hard to accept, much less embrace; yet we have been changing physically, emotionally, and spiritually since birth. Our circumstances and surroundings change day by day, even moment by moment. Think how boring life would be without change. Remember the movie *Groundhog Day*? Bill Murray had to relive the same day over and over again. He'd wake up in the morning to the same words from the radio announcer, and he'd encounter the same people who would do the same things. It was no wonder that after about a week or so of living the same day repeatedly, the guy tried to kill himself— only to wake up and start the day all over again!

It's easy to embrace the changes we plan for or expect to happen in the natural course of events—the birth of a child, for instance, or graduation from high school or college. We even look forward to change when we believe it's going to be good. Who hasn't welcomed a vacation, or a promotion at work? Who wouldn't enjoy replacing an old boxy twenty-inch television with a brand-new forty-two-inch plasma TV? But when change is unplanned, we get nervous. And when it is unexpected or negative, it's often too much for us to take. We go numb, or we wallow in our misfortune; maybe we shut down completely. We become *change resisters,* stubbornly holding on to the status quo even when it causes us pain.

In my sophomore year of college I got sick—really sick. I had made the Seattle University basketball team as a freshman. (In fact, I'd gone to Seattle U. because it offered me a complete basketball scholarship.) But I hadn't been happy with my level of play my freshman year, and I was determined to do better. The summer before sophomore year I'd practiced so hard that I'd worn my body down. The first couple of months of the fall semester I felt as if I had a never-ending case of the flu. The doctor finally diagnosed pneumonia and told me I had to rest.

This was not what I had planned for my sophomore year! I resisted the unplanned change, and I was determined to keep playing. I grudgingly followed the doctor's advice: I'd rest for a while but return to basketball practice as soon as I felt better, only to get sick again. I got over pneumonia and immediately came down with pleurisy. When I did get back on the court, I had no stamina. By midseason I'd played only a few minutes of a couple of games (and I'd had to leave the floor because I was so exhausted). Finally a specialist told me I might have sarcoidosis, a nasty inflammation that can cause permanent scarring of the affected organs (in my case, the lungs). At that point the doctor told me I had to stop trying to play. "You have to take the time to heal," he said.

I was a perfect example of what can happen to a change resister. Because I'd resisted the fact that my body just wasn't up to playing, I'd gotten sicker and sicker. I was suffering not only from physical illness but also from the malady that all change resisters contract: a crippling disease we might call change-osis. I was desperately afraid of change. Only when I embraced the change that was forced upon me could I begin to heal. I sat out the remainder of the basketball season. I continued to attend classes, but every moment I could, I rested. After five months I

began to feel better and regain my strength. The next year I was
back on the team.

FIGHTING THE FEAR
OF CHANGE

Change-osis, or the fear of change, is natural at times. Change is
often risky. It requires that we leave the familiar and strike out
into the unknown, and that creates fear. Change-osis keeps us
stagnant and complacent. Even though we know change may be
good for us, we tell people we're content. "Better the devil you
know than the devil you don't know," the old saying goes.

I saw the effects of change-osis all too clearly in my time at
IBM. IBM had always had a policy of lifetime employment. If
you were loyal to the company, the company was loyal to you. But
eventually IBM had to adjust to a new business climate and
shrinking market share. The company announced that for the
first time in its history there would be layoffs.

An awful lot of change resisters and people with change-osis
were roaming the halls of IBM back then! People who never had
considered the possibility of a job with another company had to
accept a new, uncertain reality. For the first time they were going
to have to search for a job outside of IBM. Many of these folks
had never even written a resume and had no idea how to describe
what they did at IBM in outsider's terms. Fortunately, IBM's
policy of taking care of their employees extended to people who
were being laid off. The company paid for outplacement con-
sulting for all departing employees. This helped alleviate some of
the fear and made the transition, if not easy, at least easier.

In *Who Moved My Cheese*, Spencer Johnson and Kenneth
Blanchard tell the story of mice that live in a maze and must deal
with change when someone moves their cheese. Like the charac-
ters in the maze, most human beings prefer their cheese to stay

just where it's always been, thank you very much. But in life, the cheese moves. The marketplace changes. Jobs change. Sometimes jobs even go away. What do you do then? Like the mice, you can stand in the middle of the maze and yell, "Who moved my cheese?!?" Or you can adapt to the change and get to work finding where the new cheese is hidden.

STEP OUT OF YOUR COMFORT ZONE

Embracing change usually requires that we step out of our comfort zone and do things we've never tried before. Katie London, Director of Job Development at DBM Career Services, specializes in treating change-osis. She has dealt directly with some six thousand individuals looking for jobs, usually because they've been fired, laid off, or downsized. Katie has seen every kind of reaction to change in people, but she particularly recalls one very special guy we'll call Jerry. Jerry's world had been shaken by the loss of his job. He lacked confidence, was introverted, and couldn't look people in the eye. But Katie reviewed his work accomplishments and saw that they were quite impressive. She and Jerry put together his resume and began to set up interviews. None, however, resulted in employment. Jerry's confidence was flagging, but he and Katie persisted in his job search.

In the meantime, Jerry joined a gym. That prompted Katie to tell Jerry about the personal trainer in her own gym. The trainer had told one of his clients that he was looking for a different kind of job. That client spoke with his company's human relations department and helped the trainer get an interview. One thing led to another, and the trainer was hired by his client's company.

Katie explained to Jerry that he was missing out on a big opportunity if he didn't network (i.e., connect) with people at the

> **If we want to learn and grow, we must not just accept change—we must embrace it.**

gym. She encouraged him to strike up conversations with other members. He could begin by asking people simple questions about their training goals or how long they'd been going to the gym.

Jerry took Katie's advice. He stepped out of his comfort zone and started talking to other people who were working out at his gym. Slowly, his confidence began to build. One day he met a person who worked for a company that Jerry admired. As they talked during their workouts Jerry discovered that the company had an open position that was pretty close to Jerry's dream job. The only catch was that Jerry wasn't one hundred percent qualified. He was missing one critical skill.

But Jerry refused to give up. With Katie to encourage him, Jerry continued to build a friendship with the man at the gym. This gentleman was impressed by Jerry's dedication and work ethic. He spoke up for Jerry at his company, and with the friend's endorsement, Jerry landed the job.

Most of us tend to change only when the pain of remaining the same becomes greater than the pain of changing. But in a world and a business climate of constant change, that is simply not acceptable today. Doing things the same old way will get us nowhere. If we want to keep up, we must accept changes when they come. If we want to learn and grow, we must not just accept change—we must embrace it.

OPPORTUNITY COMES FROM DIFFERENCE

The secret of embracing change and opening up to opportunities is to recognize the ways in which we are different. Think of the richness that would be lost if everyone were exactly like you!

How would you learn anything? How could you grow unless you could benefit from the differences between your life experiences and those of other people?

Even more important, we need to recognize how our differences complement one another. Did you ever notice how each panel of the beach ball is a different color and yet they're all connected? Imagine yourself as one of the panels: a "purple" person. You've always been purple, and you're comfortable around other purple people. However, one of your co-workers is very definitely green. You just cannot understand those green folks, and you're a little nervous around them. But unless you find a way to work with the green people, the "beach ball" of your workplace won't function as it was meant to.

For your business to roll smoothly along, all parts must work together. You may never fully understand the "green" guy in accounting or the "yellow" woman in sales, simply because they're not purple. But if you open yourself to the opportunities that these people have to offer, you may find that together you'll be able to accomplish great things.

WINNING WITH DIVERSITY OF THOUGHT

In today's world of business, *diversity* is one of the big buzzwords. Diversity means to accept people's differences and figure out how to work together anyway. But to my mind, diversity doesn't just mean throwing people together and hoping they can make things work. Diversity is worthless unless people are willing to open up to the different points of view that diversity brings. We don't need diversity; we need diversity of thought. Diversity without an open mind is a recipe for prejudice. With an open mind and a desire to connect, however, diversity can be a gift to help us all learn, grow, and achieve more together than we ever could achieve alone.

I recently read about another great example of diversity of thought. In Texas, high school football is king, and competition is fierce. Towns all over the state live and die on the victories or defeats of their local teams. The Dallas–Fort Worth suburb of Euless is no exception. The Euless Trinity Trojans consistently had winning seasons and frequently went to the playoffs. Twice in recent years they'd made the state semifinals in their division—but they'd never won the state championship.

Euless has one of the most ethnically diverse student bodies in the state of Texas. Caucasians, African Americans, Hispanics, Middle Easterners, Asians, Indians, and Tongans are all represented in the school and on the football team. The Tongans in particular are a dominant presence, known both for their size and for their athletic prowess.

Tonga is a small island in the South Pacific, and the Tongans share the region's Polynesian heritage. One spring some of the Tongan players were sitting in a computer lab, surfing the Internet, and came across a dance called the *haka,* a traditional tribal war dance of the Maori people in New Zealand. The Maoris are renowned Polynesian warriors, and their dance is designed to inspire ferocity in them and terror in their opponents.

The Web site depicted a New Zealand rugby team performing the *haka* dance and chant before a game. The Tongan players thought: why not do the *haka* before our football games? They practiced the moves in secret, then went to the coaching staff and asked if they could demonstrate the *haka* for the team. The ferocity of the dance, with its stomping, shouting, kicking, and jabbing, electrified the players and coaches. The entire team decided to learn the *haka* and perform it before their games.

The Euless Trinity Trojans first performed the *haka* at the beginning of their season. Just imagine the shock of the football fans at that first game, when all these good old West Texas football players dropped into a crouch and started shouting strange words and thrusting their fists into the air! But learning and performing the *haka* together did something wonderful for the team: it created unity from diversity. One of the players said, "The *haka* has brought us really close. We've had nothing but love and respect for one another, and it's shown on the field. No matter if you're Tongan, black, white, or Mexican, we're all the same at Trinity and headed toward the same goal. It's cool to see all the different cultures combine to make a championship team."

That year the Trojans won the Class 5A Division 1 state football championship. The next year they went undefeated in the regular season. They even thrashed the Odessa Permian Panthers, the state's best-known high school football powerhouse. Now Trinity Trojan football fans come to the stadium an hour early to witness the *haka*. The team has performed the dance for elementary schools, and the younger kids are learning and performing it to honor their high-school heroes. The dance also has made people in the local Tongan community feel more a part of their Texas home.

When the Trinity Trojans came together in the *haka*, they found that they cared about one another. When you care, you learn to open up to the opportunities represented by those around you, regardless of differences. Your background and preferences may be different from those of your co-worker, neighbor, or even family member. But when you open up to opportunities, you can work effectively together to accomplish a shared vision.

PEEL OFF THE LABELS

It's easy to open up to opportunities that feel familiar or when we immediately see why this is a great opening. But sometimes we just don't see any value in making a connection, so we close our minds to the opportunity it represents. And in the process, we build walls and create barriers that stand in the way of our success.

What creates these barriers and lack of connection? Biases. We all have them. However, unaddressed biases will shut down an organization and distract us from our individual purposes faster than almost anything else.

Why do we develop biases? After all, we're not born with them. If you don't believe me, watch babies or toddlers playing together. They don't care whether the other kids are white, black, brown, red, yellow, purple, or green. They don't care whether the other kids are blind or deaf or can't walk. They don't care whether the other kids are rich or poor, American or Iranian, skinny or fat. All they want are other kids to play with. But as we grow, two things happen. First, the people around us teach us their biases. If your dad played for Texas and always talked trash about Texas A&M, you'll probably grow up doing the same. Second, we tend to label anyone whom we perceive as different. A label is a destructive mental shortcut that prevents us from opening our minds and truly getting to know the rich diversity of people in this world.

My career at IBM was almost short-circuited because of a label. After eight years with the company as a marketing representative I was asked to spend two weeks as a guest sales instructor for new hires at IBM Retail Marketing Education in Atlanta, Georgia. During those two weeks I discovered I loved teaching, training, and motivating people. I decided this was what I truly wanted to do.

But over the next few years I waited to be recommended for my dream job, completed training, had my job sold out from under me, changed divisions, went through more training, changed over to a new product line, and went back for retraining. It was quite a saga. In my last position my manager at the time told me that if I supported the team at the branch, handled these few selected small accounts, and did well on my training, he'd be sure I made the 100

Percent Club (making 100 percent of my yearly sales quota), and that would help me get the promotion down the road.

I did a great job in the training, but when the managers announced which associates on the team had made the 100 Percent Club, my name wasn't among them. I was confused and a little angry. I asked why I hadn't been chosen, but no one would talk to me directly about it.

One of the managers, however, noticed that I'd been treated differently and decided to investigate. After a few weeks he came to me and said, "Keith, this is awkward, but I have to ask you some questions. Do you own a Mercedes?" I did. "Did you just go to Europe on a vacation?" I had. "Did you just build a house for yourself?" I had.

He swallowed. "Keith . . . do you sell drugs?"

You could have knocked me over with a feather. "Me, sell drugs?! No way!" I said vehemently.

My manager had the decency to look embarrassed. He told me that upper management had concluded that the only way I could have gotten the car, the vacation, and the house was if I were selling drugs. Controlling my anger, I explained very carefully that I'd used frequent flyer miles for the trip. I'd worked with a European Mercedes-Benz dealer to import three cars, which I had sold and used the profits to buy my own Mercedes at a deep discount. And the year before, I'd sold a different car and used the money to put a down payment on a lot I'd bought from my own grandmother. Once my manager passed that information along to his colleagues, I lost the label of "possible drug dealer" and my career started moving in a more positive direction.

Once we see past the labels, all kinds of opportunities lie open before us. One summer, an intern by the name of Britini came to work at Hattie Hill Enterprises while attending law school. Because Britini was young, she was labeled as inexperienced and given the

Once we see past the labels, all kinds of opportunities lie open before us.

duty of answering the phones. One day some staff members were in the conference room working on a project, and Britini surprised everyone with some valuable suggestions. It became immediately apparent that Britini thought very strategically. In that moment, her label fell off. She was seen for who she truly was, and she became a valuable member of the team for that entire summer.

WHAT ARE
YOUR LABELS?

What labels have you created in your own life? Perhaps you work with people you have labeled according to the color of their skin or ethnic background. Or perhaps you have biases about folks who are fat or rich or poor or uneducated. How do those labels affect your behavior? Imagine that you work as a loan officer in a bank. A man walks in, sits down across from you, and says, "I'd like to open a business banking account and apply for a loan." The man has a very heavy accent of some kind; you notice his clothes are untidy, and he has dirt under his fingernails. Do you immediately think that the man lacks financial resources and isn't worth your time? What if he owns a successful auto repair business down the street and wants to expand to a second location?

Perhaps you're the one walking into the bank to ask for the loan. The loan officer looks to you as if she's about twelve years old. She mentions to you that she just started at the bank last week. Do you think, "She can't know what she's doing"? But is it just possible that because of her recent training she knows more about the bank's loan products than the guy who hasn't bothered to attend a training for the past five years? What opportunity have you missed because your eyes were closed to it?

There's an old story about a martial arts master who was approached by an eager student. The student demanded of the master, "Teach me everything you know!" The master smiled and asked the student to stay for tea.

When the tea arrived, the master took the teapot and began pouring a cup for the student. He poured until the cup was full— and kept pouring. Tea overflowed the cup and splashed onto the table. The student had to jump out of the way as the hot tea streamed toward him.

"Master, what are you doing? That cup is full!" the student exclaimed.

The master looked at the student. "Just as you are filled with thoughts, ideas, prejudices, and judgments," he said. "Only when you are empty of all these can you be filled with what I have to offer."

Opening up to opportunities doesn't mean being wishy-washy or devoid of values and convictions. It does mean being open to hear the values and convictions of others. How are you ever going to connect to someone if you don't understand what makes the other person tick? To open up to opportunities, we must pause and empty ourselves of our prejudices, thoughts, labels, and judgments about others. We can't necessarily control the biases and labels of others, but we can control our own. We can learn to reprogram our thoughts so that labeling won't be a part of our mind-set. It's imperative that we do that if we are ever going to CONNECT.

PAUSE TO CONSIDER CONSEQUENCES

The labels we place on people dictate our behavior toward them. And our behavior always has impact and consequences. It either connects us to others or disconnects us from them, depending on the behavior. For example, a successful businessman we'll call Peter went to a fund-raising luncheon. Peter liked this particular cause and brought a $10,000 check with him as a donation.

When he arrived, however, the host of the fund-raiser was telling ethnic jokes—unaware that Peter's wife was from that ethnic group. As the host went on and on, Peter thought, "If this is the kind of person who represents the organization, I don't want any part of it." So he left with his donation check still in his pocket.

How could the host have prevented that type of disconnect? By pausing for what we call a *Five-Second Opportunity Detector*. It's a very simple technique. Whenever you find yourself reacting automatically and negatively toward a person, stop and pause for five seconds. Then ask yourself what the consequences might be if you say or do what you have been thinking. Who is the person behind the label? What value does he or she have to contribute? Ask yourself, "What's the opportunity here?" For instance, if the host of the fund-raiser had paused for just five seconds to think before speaking, he might have realized that there could be an ethnic person in the audience or a person with ethnic relatives or friends, and that his joke might offend them. He might have even gone deeper and remembered that if a person is of a particular race or religion, that represents only one part of the person's humanity. He might have taken the opportunity to find common ground rather than emphasizing differences. And he might have left the fund-raiser with a $10,000 donation.

In a world where technology causes things to happen in a nanosecond, pausing for five seconds sounds like an eternity. It's hard to do in our fast-paced society. But you can learn to do it. Think about what would happen if you paused for a Five-Second Opportunity Detector. How would it change your thinking? How would a change in your thinking influence your behavior? And how would the new behavior bring about positive conse-quences? The more you practice pausing before you speak, the more it will become second nature. The Five-Second Opportu-nity Detector helps you get past your own labels and prejudices to see what's truly present.

FOUR STEPS TO OPENING UP
TO OPPORTUNITIES

The Five-Second Opportunity Detector is a way to stop and readjust your thinking so you can overcome biases toward those with whom you live and work every day. Once you've paused, use these four key steps to strip away your preconceived ideas and open up to the opportunities placed in your path.

Step One. *Do a self-assessment.* Ask yourself what disturbs you about a person. Why is it that you aren't willing or able to connect? Maybe you don't like skinny women. Or it's the person's age. Or race. Be honest in your responses. Many of the labels we put on people came from the environment in which we grew up. If you heard from your friends or parents that most Latinos are illegal immigrants, for instance, you'll probably believe it's true. Or maybe you grew up in an athletic family and thought that anyone who was overweight was simply too lazy to exercise. When you discover what makes you uncomfortable about someone, it drives you to the second step.

Step Two. *Be willing to address the issue.* It is your responsibility to deal with your own biases and labels. You must address whatever bothers you about a person in two ways. First, with yourself. If that individual reminds you of someone who wronged you in the past, it's time for a reality check. Those two individuals are not one and the same. You must decide to get to know who this person really is. Second, you must address it with the other person. Even if the person's actions have caused you to label him or her "slow" or "careless" or "unthinking," and so on, you must be willing to get past the label and find out the truth. You need to move to step three.

Step Three. *Ask questions.* The best way to get to know someone is to ask questions. Everyone wants to be known and understood, so your goal is to discover what's really going on with this person. Formulate questions that will prompt conversation. Stay away from "Why" questions, such as "Why did you do such-and-such?" ("Why did you miss that deadline?"). "What" and "how" questions often work better to discover someone's thinking or emotions. "What was it like for you growing up?" "What does it mean to you to do a good job?" "How are you liking your work?" "What kind of support do you need?" These are examples of questions that will help you connect.

When I was in college, a professor once asked our class, "What are the four most important words in business?" Most of the students made jokes, saying things like "Here is your paycheck" and "Take the day off." The professor listened with a smile, then said, "The four most important words in business are 'What do you think?'" Asking for others' opinions will go a long way to removing any of your biases and labels and seeing people for who they really are. But the real key to opening up to opportunities lies in step four.

Step Four. *Be quick to listen and slow to speak.* Once you ask questions, you must truly listen to what the person has to say. Listening is the best way of learning to accept a person who is different from you. It's critical if you have any intention of succeeding as a team, an organization, or a family. Chances are that your preconceived ideas about a person will be dispelled as you listen and learn. Usually you'll find that you're more alike than different, and any differences may be a great chance for you to learn new things.

Genuine listening takes effort. How many times have you been in a conversation where the other person is talking and you're so busy thinking about how you're going to respond that you miss what is being said? What about your body language? Do you look around when someone is talking to you? Do your eyes wander, or are you fidgety? When you're on the phone, do you check e-mail at the same time? You may think you're pretty good at multitasking or feigning interest in what another person is saying. In reality, the other person almost always can tell when you are not fully engaged.

You will never build trust or truly connect with an individual until you learn the art of active listening. The other person needs to feel that there is nothing more important to you than what he or she is saying. You can convey that message by asking follow-up questions to probe even deeper. Drill down past the superficial level. Ask people to expand when they make a statement or to explain what something means to them. Take the time to listen, and you will open up to opportunities as you learn the needs, wants, desires, and dreams of individuals. And above all, be authentic. Don't just go through the motions. Listen because you care about what this person has to say.

My mentor Bob Moawad once remarked, "One of the best ways we can show people they are genuinely important to us is to give them our undivided attention." Successful businesses are those whose leaders and employees have learned to listen to one another and to their customers. When you employ these skills, you will be transformed from an average listener to an active listener. People will drop their defenses and open up, and you'll discover the well of goodness that lies inside every human being.

LEADING BY LISTENING

It's one thing to transform from a change resister to a change embracer and to see change as an opportunity for growth. But how do you help others open up to opportunities? For business leaders, that is an ongoing challenge. Communicating and preparing people for change can help alleviate any fear and anxiety, but you also must open up to the opportunity of hearing the concerns of others. Trust and connection are built through dialogue and an open exchange of ideas.

As Director of Worldwide Sales Training and Development at

Ortho Clinical Diagnostics (a division of Johnson & Johnson), Dave Manning used the power of listening and communicating to ensure the success of one of the biggest product launches the company had ever seen. In many companies the upper echelons make most of the decisions about product rollouts. But Dave saw the importance of gathering input from the sales force that would deliver the new product.

Every day for six months, Dave carved an hour out of his busy schedule to call a manager or sales rep and ask about their needs and expectations for the product rollout. He then spent a week in each sales region across the company for face-to-face meetings. On the basis of this input, Dave and his team put together strategies for the product launch.

Dave Manning connected to those involved with the project by seeking their input and actively listening. He conveyed to individuals within the sales force that what they had to say was of value, making them feel comfortable enough to voice their opinions. Dave heard the wisdom they shared and implemented many of their ideas. When the sales teams started promoting the new product, their numbers far exceeded expectations, and the entire organization was energized by the product's success.

LISTENING TO GUESTS AND EMPLOYEES

Rob Smith, General Manager of the Wyndham Aruba Resort, Spa & Casino, makes a special effort to hear from both his hotel guests and his employees. For almost ten years, Rob has set aside one hour two days a week to sit at a lobby desk and talk with hotel guests about any nonurgent matters. (Of course, guests can also contact him at any other time, too.) As a result of his availability, Rob has learned invaluable information. Guests often approach him at that lobby desk to praise hotel employees. If guests have problems, they get the assurance of the hotel manager that those problems will be resolved. While resort hotels typically receive several guest complaint letters, the Wyndham Aruba Resort receives very few. According to Rob, those two hours he spends in the hotel lobby each week make all the difference.

Rob's open door policy extends to hotel employees. He made himself even more accessible by moving his office from the executive area to the back of the hotel, across from the employee cafeteria. He also spends an hour of each week sitting at a desk in the receiving area where employees come in every day, giving them an opportunity to share their thoughts and comments. Rob listens to employees. He takes the time to get to know them and listen to their concerns. Consequently, those employees stick around, as is evidenced by a turnover at the resort of less than one percent.

CAN YOU HEAR ME NOW?

Jim McGean, president of the south area of Verizon Wireless, believes in the company's advertising slogan, "Can you hear me now?" Every quarter, he leads several "All Hands" meetings where he interacts with two thousand of the three thousand Georgia/Alabama employees. During those meetings, Jim talks about the mission, the region's quarterly results, and future action items. But according to Jim, the most important part of each meeting is the question-and-answer session at the end. Employees can ask anything, and the managers do their best to answer these questions fully.

Throughout the year, Jim sets up a series of "listening posts," where he talks with customers and employees outside of normal channels. Regular departmental meetings include cross-sectional roundtables, where Jim speaks for five minutes and then listens for an hour. Jim's open door policy doesn't stop there: he also makes in-store visits and takes time for one-on-one sessions with employees.

The result is that the Georgia/Alabama region consistently and significantly contributes to the overall success of Verizon Wireless. The company has outpaced the rest of the telecommunications industry, with fourteen consecutive quarters of double-digit year-over-year net customer growth. Verizon Wireless is the only carrier to balance revenue growth and customer growth simultaneously. The company attributes its success to focusing on the fundamentals—the best, most reliable network; a vast array of products and services; and highest customer loyalty in the industry—all fueled by award-winning customer service. It's pretty clear that the basis of that great customer service is a willingness of managers like Jim McGean to listen to both customers and employees.

Dave Manning, Rob Smith, and Jim McGean are not just open to the opportunity to listen to their employees and customers. They *create* opportunities. They proactively seek chances to hear from others and change the status quo based on the information they receive. Great leaders like these gentlemen are always looking for opportunities to change things for the better. We all can learn something from the stories of their success.

THREE MASTER KEYS TO OPEN UP TO OPPORTUNITIES AND EMBRACE CHANGE

Three master keys will help you open up to opportunities and be a change embracer. The first is to *face the change without fear*. Sure, the change is real and may be challenging, but the negative implications you associate with change may be temporary or even an illusion.

Let's take a worst-case scenario: you get the news that you are being downsized. Suddenly, you are jobless. Your first reaction is panic. You can feel stress gripping your mind and body. You think that no one will ever want to employ you again. You envision a future of poverty and begin to question your value in the workplace (or worse yet, your value as a human being). That's when you need to do a simple reality check. Ask yourself the following questions.

1. What's the truth? What's the reality here?

The truth is that you weren't fired for not doing your job; your job simply disappeared. The truth is that your supposed future as a homeless person is false evidence. The reality is that you need a new job. The reality is that lots of jobs are out there for which you're suited; you just have to start looking.

2. What could be good about this? What's the opportunity?

If you look hard enough, there is opportunity in almost every change. What could be good about losing your job is that you now can get a better one. What could be good is that you never might have looked outside of your company to see what else is out there if you hadn't been downsized. Now you might have the opportunity to learn new skills, meet new people, and even take a new career or life direction.

Once you've asked these questions, take a deep breath and decide to embrace the change. Go so far as to celebrate it. Then take action to get a new and even better job—one that will bring you greater fulfillment and open up new opportunities.

The second master key to opening up to opportunities is to *open your heart.* We all possess a spirit that binds us together, regardless of our differences. It's what we call the spirit factor. Another word for it is empathy. That means to take on the feelings and experiences of others as if they are our own. It's as if a switch is turned on within us that shines a light, enabling us to see into the soul and spirit of another human being.

The spirit factor connects us to total strangers. Remember what it was like to watch the people who were stranded in New Orleans in the wake of Hurricane Katrina? Even if you'd never been to New Orleans and never known anyone who lived there, didn't you feel upset and angry over the horrific circumstances those people endured? When disaster strikes, we don't think about people's race, gender, age, or lifestyle. We see people just like us. If we see a car accident on the road or if someone in front of us falls, we will drop our preconceived ideas and negative thoughts to reach out and lend a hand. We all know what it's like to be in trouble and need help. And we instinctively reach across our differences to embrace both the changes and the opportunities that we might otherwise have ignored.

If this need to connect emerges in the light of dramatic events, doesn't it stand to reason that the need is always there? Why is it that it takes a tragedy to strip away the biases and defenses we layer on? Why is it that we have a co-worker we don't like, but the moment their home burns down or they lose a child, we are immediately connected? How can we learn to connect to others in the normalcy of our day-to-day lives?

We must realize that while the events surrounding us may have changed and the drama may have subsided, the core things that bind us together remain. The spirit factor exists within each of us. When we discover the spirit factor that binds us together, we discover the value in what others have to contribute. If we want to stay connected to people, we must look for and recognize that spirit factor: the things we share in common. When we recognize our similarities we will open up to opportunities and embrace change far more easily.

The third master key is this: *you must believe.* You must believe that something good is going to happen to you. You must believe, you must believe, you must believe. Keep your expectations high and your faith strong. This isn't pie-in-the-sky advice. It is a true antidote to change-osis—one that works. It starts with facing the change without fear. Remember who you are and that you are worthy of great things. A world of opportunity is now open to you. When you face the change without fear and discover the reality of your situation, you are on the road to embracing change rather than resisting it.

When we connect to these three master keys, we begin to change from within. It's the kind of change that will empower us to deal with, and even embrace, the people in our lives whom we don't understand or who might rub us the wrong way. Someone once said, "The only thing you can change is yourself, but sometimes that changes everything." When we change from the inside and begin to understand the value in connecting to people, we will open to opportunities. Sometimes that happens naturally as life experience automatically connects us. More often than not, it takes work. We must make an effort to listen and hear beneath the surface to understand people's needs. But with that effort comes great reward. We accomplish our goals, we learn to embrace change enthusiastically, and we inspire the same enthusiasm in others. As a result, we find that we have transformed our lives for the better.

OPEN UP TO OPPORTUNITIES ACTION STEPS

1. How can you open up to the opportunities that come into your life? What must you do to in order to overcome your fears? What beliefs must you adopt? Whom must you connect with?

2. How have you dealt with change in the past? Did you resist it or embrace it? Think of a time when you

embraced a change in your life. It could be a graduation, the birth of a child, a new job—anything. How did it feel?

3. Now, think of a specific instance when you resisted change. What was the ultimate outcome? Did the change happen anyway? How could you have embraced the change, and what would have been the result?

4. Opening up to opportunities means examining your biases and the labels you attach to others. What biases and labels have prevented you from accepting people and situations? How can you benefit from embracing diversity?

5. Remember a time when you said something you wish you hadn't because you offended or upset someone unintentionally. How could the Five-Second Opportunity Detector have helped you avoid your mistake?

6. To get past biases and labels, use the four steps in this chapter. First, do a self-assessment. Second, be willing to address the issue. Third, ask questions. Fourth, listen! If you had taken these four steps in the situation you described, how would the outcome have been different?

7. The next time you're with someone or talking on the phone, practice active listening. Don't allow yourself to get distracted or try to multitask. Truly listen to the other person and respond with your whole heart and mind.

8. As a leader in business, how can you use active listening to help yourself and others institute and embrace change?

9. Are you facing a change right now? If so, what fears are coming up? The first master key to embracing change is to *face the change without fear.* Take yourself through

the reality check process. Ask yourself, "What's the truth? What's the reality here?"

10. Now, ask yourself the second set of reality check questions: "What could be good about this? What's the opportunity?" How could you embrace this change in your life?

11. The second master key to embracing change is to *open your heart*. When have you felt compassion for someone? What can you do to create that connection with people you don't know or perhaps don't like?

12. The third master key is this: *you must believe* in yourself and in the possibility that good will come from this change. What expectations can you have that will help you believe in the best possible outcome?

13. Fill in the blank: **ICARE to take action now by doing**

_____

to open up to opportunities and be a change embracer.

CONNECT Step 3:
Notice What's Needed and Do What's Necessary

The opportunity that God sends
does not wake him who is asleep.
—*African proverb*

I had a hard time in elementary school. I had a bad stutter when I was asked to read out loud in the class, and some of the other kids took great delight in making fun of me. I was pretty good in sports and really wanted to shine in school, but I was shy and nervous in front of my peers. It didn't help that I was a lot taller than the other kids, which made me stick out like a sore thumb. Whenever our teachers lined up the students to go to an assembly or fire drill or recess, they'd always put me in the back of the line because I was the tallest.

When I entered fifth grade, I was fortunate to have a great teacher, Mr. Twine. At a time when there weren't a lot of men teaching elementary school, Mr. Twine was a great role model for me. He was strict but fair, and I felt he had high standards and really wanted us to succeed.

While I wanted to do well in class, I still lacked self-confidence.

Somehow Mr. Twine saw my burning desire and my shyness. On the first day our fifth-grade class was to march out to an assembly, he announced, "All right, everyone, form a single line behind Keith!"

He took me aside and told me, "Keith, because you're the tallest you're going to lead us. Everyone can see you. I'll be in the back of the line to make sure everyone stays together." I led the class out to that assembly with pride.

It was a very small and simple thing that Mr. Twine did, but to me it made all the difference. My confidence grew by leaps and bounds, not just because I was leading my classmates but mainly because Mr. Twine had noticed me and responded to my needs.

Notice what's needed and do what's necessary is the third CONNECT principle. We spoke in the previous chapter about the importance of listening to others. However, noticing what's needed goes beyond just listening. It starts by responding to *all* the signals you get from your team, your boss, your customers, and yourself. Noticing what's needed means that you have to get outside of your own head and step into the mind-set of others. It's being aware of the basic needs of every human being and doing your best to supply those needs before people ask for them, not afterward.

Noticing what's needed is the first step. Next, you must do what's necessary, which I define as (1) what's required in the moment and (2) what will make the biggest difference. Mr. Twine noticed that I truly wanted to do well but I was shy. He noticed that I needed more confidence. What was required in the moment was to give me an opportunity to step up in front of my classmates. My success in doing so would make the biggest difference. So he took the necessary action of having me lead my classmates to the assembly.

It's no good just to notice what's needed without doing something about it. Noticing what's needed and doing what's necessary means that you must be proactive. You must do what's necessary in the moment to make the biggest difference in the situation at hand. Your team may need motivation, and what's necessary in the moment is a pep talk or a figurative kick in the pants. Your employees may need a reward for

It's no good to notice what's needed without doing something about it.

their hard work, and what's necessary in the moment is a staff lunch on you or perhaps an award for the team's top performer. Your customers may need to feel that their input is being heard and adopted by the company, and what's necessary is a page on your Web site where you itemize all the changes that have been made on the basis of customer suggestions. Or perhaps what's necessary is a small gift or discount for any customer whose suggestion is adopted. The result of noticing what's needed and doing what's necessary will be a strong team, happier employees, a more productive workplace, and more deeply satisfied customers.

BE AWARE OF OTHERS' NEEDS

Noticing what's needed and doing what's necessary is not rocket science—so why is it that we constantly need to be reminded of this basic people skill? We get so busy or so wrapped up in our own goals and agendas that we forget to stop and notice the person next to us. If we're so busy that we're not aware of a child playing in the driveway and nearly run him over, then something is wrong. We can become so focused on our own agendas that we tune out what is happening around us every day. We can fail to be aware of what's necessary to keep our relationships healthy.

To notice what's needed and do what's necessary, we need the third BE-Attitude: we must *be aware*. When you're driving in the car, are you aware of someone waiting to cross the street? Do you stop and let the person by? Are you aware of the elderly person in the elevator and let him or her step out before you? When you walk into the office, do you make a beeline for the coffee and then go straight to your desk? Or do you stop and comment on a co-worker's new haircut? Do you ever notice the family pictures someone has on his desk? Do you ask questions about the people you work with and live beside? Do you ever ask about a co-worker's family or outside interests, or even if she is having a good day? Do you ever take the time to talk across the fence to your neighbors? How about opening the gate and asking them over? Do you do what's necessary to CONNECT with others?

Everyone has a story, and if you take the time to listen you might find it fascinating. You might discover someone in need—someone you can help, or perhaps someone who can help you. When you take the time to be aware, notice those around you, and do what's necessary, you'll be amazed at how easy it is to CONNECT.

LEADERS TUNE IN

Leaders notice what's needed and then do what's necessary. They tune in to their team, their employees, and their customers. If you hold a leadership position and learn to notice what's needed and do what's necessary for those in your workforce, you are sure to see increased loyalty and improved performance.

BethAnn Neynaber, former Area General Manager at Chilton Credit Reporting, had an employee who was late to work every day. But rather than letting the employee go, BethAnn sat her down and said, "Tell me about what brings you to work late." BethAnn discovered that the woman had to take two buses to get to work. If her babysitter was late, she would miss the bus. BethAnn offered to let the woman start work at 8:30 instead of

8:00. The employee was overjoyed and said that by working from 8:30 to 5:30, she could have all the reports done in the evenings before she left instead of waiting until the next morning.

BethAnn could have made countless assumptions or even let the woman go, losing a valuable employee. Instead, she was aware, noticed the woman's needs, and then responded with what was necessary—flexibility in accommodating her schedule. The company retained a superior employee whose performance actually improved because BethAnn had noticed what was needed and done what was necessary in the situation.

In some cases it takes an outsider to notice what's needed. One day an ISO 9000 auditor came to a local plant to inspect a manufacturing line. (ISO 9000 is a series of international standards ensuring quality management practices in business-to-business dealings.) While standing alongside a line worker, the auditor noticed that the employee's task involved contact with a very hot surface.

The auditor asked the worker, "Isn't that incredibly hot?"

"Yes. I just don't think my supervisors understand how much I need protective gloves," the worker replied.

"Has your supervisor ever been on the line with you?"

"No."

The auditor left, returned with the supervisor, and had him stand on the line to observe the employee. The next day the worker had protective gloves.

It sounds preposterous that a supervisor would never physically observe the line workers. But how many of us make assumptions or are unaware of others' needs because we keep our distance from people at work? We don't get actively involved with folks on our team. As a result, we don't notice the little things that can make the biggest difference, and we fail to do what's necessary to produce superior results.

NOTICING PLUS ACTION = "WOW"

Ed Doherty, whom you met in an earlier chapter, is a master of noticing what's needed and doing what's necessary. The result is what he calls a "wow" experience in every one of the sixty-plus Applebee's, Chevys Fresh Mex, and Panera Bread Bakery-Café franchise restaurants he owns today. In fact, the mission of Doherty Enterprises, Inc., is to "wow" the guests, employees, communities, and suppliers.

"Wow" happens by noticing what's needed and doing what's necessary, and it starts at the top. When Ed visits his restaurants, it's easy for him to say hello to the servers, hosts, and cashiers because they are out front, smiling and interacting with customers. But Ed also walks into the kitchen and greets every cook and dishwasher. He puts his hand on their shoulders and says, "You're doing a great job. Thank you." Ed feels that he and the dishwasher are just the same—Ed's just the guy who happens to write the checks.

This high level of attention extends to the communities where his restaurants are located. For example, all Applebee's restaurants create a neighborhood feeling by filling one wall of each restaurant with memorabilia from local high schools and other community organizations. But as far as Ed's concerned, one wall isn't enough. Before one of his restaurants opens for business in a new area, representatives from Ed's company go to the schools and local organizations to introduce themselves. They collect memorabilia to display throughout the restaurant, not just on one wall. When guests come to an Ed Doherty Applebee's, they see elements of their community almost everywhere they look. That special touch personalizes the dining experience, shows respect for Applebee's customers, and creates a community "wow."

At Ed's Applebee's restaurants, employees are aware of guests before they even make it from the parking lot to the front door.

Instead of waiting until the customers enter the restaurant, the hosts open the door, greeting guests with a smile and saying, "Good morning. How are you?" or "Good afternoon. Great day, isn't it?" As they lead customers to their tables, the hosts initiate conversation, perhaps complimenting the scarf or tie a guest is wearing. The servers pay special attention to their customers' needs throughout the meal. If the customer pays by credit card, the server takes the time to read the customer's name on the card. Then, when they bring the receipt to the table, the servers say "thank you" and use the guest's name. These little touches play a big role in making customers feel special. By noticing the small things that connect, Ed Doherty's restaurant teams create long-term customer loyalty and big profits. And the customers' smiles feel good to the employees, too!

NOTICING TOO LATE

Companies that don't notice their customers or employees will certainly become aware when the good ones walk away. When Arie went to work for a major data processing company, she was promised a director position if she produced the right numbers. Well, she blew the numbers off the chart—but the promotion didn't come. The corporation said she had to wait.

Nevertheless, Arie continued to do an outstanding job. She noticed a need within the company and took the initiative to open a whole new division for outsourcing to India. Everyone considered her a shining star, but there was no promotion. Arie had a frank talk with the company's human relations manager, saying she wouldn't be around long unless the promised promotion came through. Still, nothing happened.

So Arie accepted a new job with another company. When she announced her resignation, management threw offers at her and begged her to stay. They poured out the compliments, telling her how much they valued her—but they had noticed too late. Arie left, and today she is putting her considerable talents to work for someone else.

Noticing too late can result in serious consequences. If you notice changes in your health too late and don't do what's necessary, you can develop a serious illness. If you don't notice what's needed in your relationship or do what's necessary until it's too late, your significant other can walk out the door. If you don't notice what's needed in your job and do what's necessary, you might be fired. If you're a manager and you don't notice what's needed and do what's necessary in your department, you might lose valuable employees or miss your goals.

While there might be consequences if you notice too late, it is never too late to be aware and start noticing. Do an assessment of how well you notice others. What are you saying to them? How are you acting toward them? Do you notice only when something's wrong? Or do you notice when people accomplish something great and then acknowledge them for it? And how are you at noticing your own needs?

Noticing is the first thing. Once you are aware of others' needs, however, you must then do what's necessary. Many times what's needed is very specific: a different work schedule in the case of the single mother, for example, or keeping the promise of a promotion for Arie, or even something as simple as a pair of protective gloves for the line worker. But each action should create one of three specific feelings in yourself and others: *self-worth, care,* and *respect.* When people feel that they have worth, they are cared for and about, and they are respected, then you have an atmosphere in which connection is natural and performance will soar.

DISCOVERING YOUR TRUE WORTH

We've all seen the MasterCard commercials featuring two or three activities or items, like a European vacation or a catcher's mitt, and the accompanying costs. The last scene emphasizes the memories made on that vacation or the relationship created when a father and son play catch in the backyard—something that has emotional value. A single word then appears on the screen: "Priceless."

Some things are of such immense value that no amount of money can purchase them and no dollar amount can describe their worth. You fall into that category. Whether you believe it or not, you are priceless. Your value extends far beyond silver and gold.

Too many of us put too great a value on material things. We think that having the right car or the right clothes or the right house means we're worthwhile. In and of themselves, there is nothing wrong with those things. Having a nice car, nice clothes, and a nice house are great. The right job can be very fulfilling. The right relationships can enrich our lives beyond almost anything else. The problem occurs when our identity gets wrapped up in those things—when we let them define who we are. Could it be that we are filling our lives with things and seeking status in the eyes of others to cover our own lack of self-worth?

Maybe your self-worth is high. You are confident in who you are, and you understand your purpose in life. If so, that's terrific. But even the most confident among us have moments of doubt when we're dissatisfied with a particular situation or when we feel we're on the wrong path. We need to remember that all life has its mountaintops and valleys. We can shorten our stay in the valleys by reminding ourselves of some basic truths. You have value simply because you were born upon this earth. And if you're smart, you'll be aware of and appreciate the enormous gifts you already have in your life.

Think about your ability to see. How much would you give for your eyes? If you're able to get up in the morning and walk, think about someone who is a quadriplegic. How much would you give for your legs? Even those who are in the most reduced circumstances have value and worth. How much is your life worth to you? Every breath you take is priceless. Take a fresh look at who you are and who you were created to be. How do you value who you are? How do you value what you've accomplished? How do you value being on this earth?

Feeling good about ourselves is the first step in being able to notice what's needed in other people. When your life is going well and you feel happy and optimistic, how much easier is it to help and take care of others? And if you're going through a bad patch—you just lost your job or messed up a project at work, or your spouse is really angry with you—do you notice other people's feelings or focus on your own misery? Sure, we've seen "martyrs" who give everything to other people while completely ignoring their own emotional and physical needs, but that's a recipe for resentment and burnout. To care for others, you must care for yourself. I suggest you do it sooner rather than later.

WHAT DO YOU LIKE
ABOUT YOURSELF?

If your self-worth isn't as strong as you would like, perhaps a look into your own past will explain why. Negative words and experiences or a lack of care in childhood definitely make their imprint. But I'm not one of those who believe that we are irrevocably shaped by our past. What's past cannot be changed, but the present and the future are ours to do with as we like. As someone once said, "It's never too late to have a happy childhood." To me that means I can decide today to shape my life with positive input rather than negative. At every moment, I can give myself

permission to feel good instead of lousy, no
matter what the circumstances.

People who have heard me speak know
that one of my attitude takeaways is "Never
let anyone steal your joy." That to me is the

**Never let anyone
steal your joy.**

key to keeping my attitude positive and my self-worth strong.
Recently I was in the Atlanta airport connecting from one flight
to another. Now, if you change planes in Atlanta you'd better be
prepared to hustle! There are six terminals, and inevitably when
you land at one your connecting flight is in the terminal at the
other end of the airport.

On this particular day I landed at Terminal A. My flight had
been delayed, and I knew I was going to have to run to catch my
next plane in Terminal D. I grabbed my carry-on and sprinted to
the train that goes between terminals. As soon as the doors
opened, I ran up the escalator and dashed for the gate. I went
straight up to the agent and said, "Did I make it?"

"Yep," she replied, looking tired. "But the flight's been canceled."

I'd just busted a lung for nothing! I stared at the woman and
she stared back at me, expecting me to explode. I'm sure she'd
already dealt with a lot of angry passengers that evening. Instead,
I gave her a big smile and shook my head. "I'm not going to let
you steal my joy!" I told her. I started to shake my hands as if I
were shaking water off of them. "I'm gonna shake all this negativity right off me, 'cause I'm not gonna let *anything* steal my joy!"
I said with a laugh.

The gate agent looked at me for a moment. Then she smiled
too and started shaking her own hands, shaking off the negativity
and repeating, "Flight's been canceled!" We laughed together as
we filled ourselves up with joy.

Building self-worth through positive experiences is easy once
you decide to make it a priority. Start by being nice to yourself!
All too often we can spend a lot of time focused on all the ways

we imagine we aren't as good as other people. We're conditioned to be critical and to play down our accomplishments. For example, when someone gives you a compliment, how do you respond? I can't tell you how often I've said to someone, "You did a great job," and heard the response "It was nothing" or "I messed up on one section" or "You're too kind." We're afraid that we'll look arrogant or self-important if we acknowledge how great we are. But we need to remember that self-worth is not arrogance; it's simply recognizing our value as human beings and giving credit when credit's due.

Here's a simple exercise to help you be aware of and improve your sense of self-worth.

1. On a sheet of paper, write down a minimum of seven things that you like about yourself. These can be physical characteristics, accomplishments, and character traits—anything that you consider positive. For example: "I like my nose." "I'm good to my dog." "I won the spelling bee for my school in sixth grade." "I like people." You might write, "I go long periods of time without eating junk food." Or "I can work out or run a long distance." Or "I'm an organized person." Or "I know how to be independent."

2. Now write down seven positive things that other people say about you. Have you been told that your eyes sparkle? That you're always in a good mood? That you're a self-starter? Perhaps you're good with numbers, or you're reliable, or you give others a hand. If you have trouble coming up with this list, write down ten things you imagine other people might say about you and you just didn't hear them.

3. Take this list and read each of the statements aloud. This may make you uncomfortable. If so, great! You need to learn to accept that all these great things are a part of who you are.

4. Reread the list aloud, only this time do it with enthusiasm.
    Read it as if you were celebrating a day in which you dem-
    onstrated all these great things. Read it as if you embodied
    these qualities and accomplishments and see how great it
    feels.

WHY WERE YOU BORN?

If you still have trouble finding something positive about yourself, then remember that each human being comes into the world
with unique gifts. You were born gifted. You were a gifted child.
And you are a gifted adult. We all have innate talents. You have
been called, chosen, and appointed with a gift. The question is
this: are you sitting on your gift or are you expanding it?

The two greatest moments in your life are the day you were
born and the day you discover *why* you were born. So, why were
you born? One way to answer that question is to ask yourself
what you enjoy doing. What makes your heart sing? It can be
little things, and they don't have to be career oriented. Maybe
you are a good listener, or you are very punctual. Maybe you
love teaching others. Maybe you love to learn. Maybe you're
a great connector, or great with detail. Those traits can serve
you well in a job or career, but they will also serve you well in
life. Maybe you play the piano and can use that gift to bring joy
to others. There are a myriad of ways in which we are all
gifted.

Thinking about the positive characteristics and abilities others
have recognized in you or that you recognize in yourself will help
you be aware of your gifts. When you learn to look in the mirror
and see something positive, to recognize that you are made in the
image of greatness and that you have a unique gift and purpose,
your sense of self-worth will grow. And once you have a solid

foundation of self-esteem, it will be easier to be aware of those around you and esteem them too.

RAISING SELF-WORTH RAISES PERFORMANCE

Paul Manning is in the business of building self-worth. A graduate of Virginia Tech with a degree in electrical engineering, Paul was on the fast track to success in corporate America when he got a letter in the mail that would change the course of his life. Paul's twin sister sent him an article about two of his high school friends who had murdered Paul's former next-door neighbor in a crack cocaine drug deal. Paul was devastated by the news. Worse yet, he realized that the crack cocaine epidemic was destroying inner-city African-American young men nationwide.

Rather than merely shrugging his shoulders in despair over the problem, Paul was compelled to do something about it. He decided to work with at-risk youth in the inner city of Richmond, Virginia. Paul left his engineering job to start a ministry by the name of U-TURN, Inc. Working through the Parks and Recreation Department, he grabbed kids off the basketball courts and trained them to play tennis. Why tennis? Paul wanted to create an entire shift in attitude, building self-respect in kids who had little or none. He wanted them to see beyond the confines of the ten-block radius in which they lived. Instead of playing basketball on an inner-city court, where they were expected to be, Paul wanted to give these kids opportunities to play tennis in the suburbs at exclusive country clubs.

Within a year and a half, U-TURN athletes had become so skilled that they were winning state tennis tournaments in Virginia, Maryland, West Virginia, and Washington, D.C. For the first time, these inner-city kids were seeing nice homes and manicured golf courses, and playing at private clubs, some of which only five years earlier hadn't allowed minorities to be members.

The U-TURN kids might not have fit in at the country clubs when it came to their clothing and appearance. But when it came to their skill level, they outperformed everyone they met. Kids and parents at the country clubs started asking why the U-TURN youth were such exceptional tennis players. The suburban teens and preteens wanted to get involved with the group.

They were welcomed into U-TURN with open arms. Paul understood that all kids, regardless of their race or socioeconomic background, struggle with issues of self-worth. Through sports, Paul created an environment where kids learned physical and mental discipline. He also taught that each of them had value and was uniquely gifted.

Of course, not every kid immediately took to Paul's self-worth program. It can take a while for people to start to really believe that they are of value and have purpose. When an inner-city kid is holding a trophy in her hands at a country club where the initiation fee is $50,000 to $70,000, how does that reality coincide with the fact that she is living beside a crack house and will hear gunshots when she goes home that night? Paul continually combats the detrimental influences in the kids' lives with words of affirmation. He and his program show these kids what is possible.

Adrienne is a living example of someone who turned her life around under Paul's guidance. At the age of eleven, Adrienne had been training at U-TURN for two years. Paul had taken the time to learn about her background and understand her on a deep level. Paul had noticed that Adrienne's identity, confidence, and self-esteem were based entirely on her performance on the tennis court. But he also knew that one day she would no longer be able to play at the same level. Injury or age would eventually get the better of her. Her self-worth had to be rooted in something greater and more lasting than sports.

One day, he and Adrienne were talking about issues of self-esteem. He said to her, "Adrienne, I bet you can't look at yourself in the mirror for more than fifteen seconds."

"Yes, I can," she said.

"Well, do it," he challenged.

Adrienne boldly fixed her eyes on the mirror in front of her—but could hold her gaze for only about five seconds. She then dropped her head and turned away.

"Why can't I look at myself with confidence? Why am I not happy with what I see in the mirror?" Adrienne asked.

Paul told her, "Stop listening to what society or other people might say about you. Listen to God's voice instead. You are loved, you are special, and you have a purpose." It took time, but Adrienne took Paul's words to heart and was transformed. You'll hear more about this remarkable young woman's story in a later chapter.

CARE AND CAPTURE HEARTS

While I was working on this book I received an e-mail from a corporation asking me to come in and speak. "Hopefully you can have an impact on upper management," my correspondent wrote. "All of us worked hard when we felt cared for. We hope you can help bring that feeling back."

Caring is the second essential feeling that's needed by everyone. People in the workplace don't generally talk about making someone feel cared for. Yet caring creates harmony, peace, tolerance, and acceptance of diversity in the workplace. Human needs don't stop just because you walk into an office on Monday morning. People want to feel cared for and to know that their opinions hold merit. We all want to be understood and accepted. We are relational beings regardless of the role we are playing at any given moment—whether we are at home, in the workplace, or in a social setting.

Pam McNair-Wingate understands the power of caring for

those around her. As owner of Gadabout Salon & Day Spas, Pam operates seven salons and spas in the Tucson, Arizona, area. Pam believes in nurturing ideas, people, and environments. She does that by noticing what's needed and doing what's necessary. "People want to know that their employer is interested in them as human beings—not as a piece of equipment that comes in on a daily basis, does a job, and leaves," she told us. "Building a culture and community in which people feel safe to be who they are makes a workplace passionately important in someone's life instead of just a place to show up."

Fifty-six of three hundred employees have been with Gadabout for more than ten years—an astounding length of time in the salon industry. If you were to ask any of those employees why, they would more than likely tell you it's because they feel cared for. Gadabout connects with people in a way that captures their hearts, which in turn creates a higher level of loyalty. Pam McNair-Wingate recognizes all employees' birthdays with cards and gift certificates. Every year on their anniversary with the salon, employees get roses.

Pam also makes her employees feel special by catching them doing things right. If employees come in and serve an extra client or regularly show up for work on time, Pam lets them know they are appreciated. Twice a year, she recognizes those who have not been late or absent by giving them an extra vacation day.

The special effort to notice others doesn't stop with her employees. The first Gadabout Salon opened its doors twenty-five years ago, and for three months every client that came through the door received a rose, signifying the unique beauty of the individual. If a client forgot to take her rose, someone from the salon—often Pam herself—drove to that person's home to deliver the flower. Recently Gadabout celebrated its twenty-fifth anniversary by once again distributing roses—this time to some seventeen thousand clients. As Pam says, "It's about nurturing clients." Nurturing, or caring, makes for loyal customers and greatly expanded business.

UNEXPECTED DELIGHTS

Hampton Inn goes out of its way to make hotel guests feel cared for. The hotel chain employees have been trained in a program called Moment Makers. "Moments" occur when an employee makes a momentary connection with a guest through empathy, through humor, or by creating unexpected delights. If a guest walks in out of the rain looking frazzled, for instance, the desk clerk might say, "It sure looks like you've had a bad day. Let me get you checked in here as quickly as I can." That approach is far more personal than uttering, "Your credit card, please."

Another such moment might occur when a hotel maintenance man notices that it snowed in the middle of the night and at 5:00 in the morning takes it upon himself to brush off all the car windshields in the parking lot. Or if it's a hot, muggy day in the middle of the summer, a pitcher of lemonade at the front desk works wonders in letting guests know that Hampton Inn cares about their needs. Hampton Inn has learned how to create an experience that connects employees to customers, creating memorable moments that produce return business and greater satisfaction all around.

SHOW AN INTEREST IN OTHERS

When managers and leaders in an organization notice the needs and the contributions of the people they lead, it inspires co-workers to notice one another. The result is a workforce that feels cared for and therefore connected. Caring about others means noticing who they are. What is someone's life like when he or she leaves the office? What do they care about? When you care about those around you, you will naturally be curious to know who they are and ask questions to find out. Ask about their home life, their families, their hobbies—without being intrusive, of course. But if people sense that you truly want to know them, they will usually be more than willing to share.

> **Caring about others means noticing who they are.**

In *How to Win Friends and Influence People*, Dale Carnegie advises, "Become genuinely interested in other people . . . Be a good listener. Encourage people to talk about themselves . . . Talk in terms of the other person's interests . . . Make the other person feel important—and do it sincerely." Seven decades later, his book is still a household staple, and people flock to Dale Carnegie courses. That's because human beings understand that the most important thing we can do is to care and connect with others.

I LIKE YOU BECAUSE . . .

One of the most important ways we can show people we care is by telling them. Mother Teresa said, "Kind words can be short and easy to speak, but their echoes are truly endless." Mark Twain put it another way, saying, "I can live for two months on one good compliment." We all need compliments. We all need to know that we are noticed and appreciated and our efforts are recognized. When you take a moment to notice someone's greatness and tell him or her about it, you give a gift that will always be remembered.

For more than twenty-five years, Zig Ziglar Training Systems has held "Born to Win" seminars. In the course of the program, attendees recognize others' positive attributes and write personal notes to one another, beginning with the words, "I like you because. . ." It could be something simple like "I like you because you smiled at me." Or "I like you because you asked about my family." At the end of a program, people feel really good about themselves.

Three women who met at one "Born to Win" session made such a strong connection that they decided to share a final meal together. They were fortunate to get a table at a nice restaurant nearby. Everything about the dining experience was perfect, including the waiter, who provided outstanding service. The women chose to leave a thirty percent tip on a very expensive meal.

Then one woman said to the others, "Wait a minute! What did we just learn about the power of positive words? Let's leave our waiter more than just the tip." They tore a sheet of paper into three pieces, and each woman wrote the waiter a personal note that began, "I like you because..." The ladies left the tip and the notes and went out the front door.

Before they had gotten to their cars, they heard a voice from the restaurant—"Wait up! Wait up!" They turned and saw the waiter running toward them, waving the pieces of paper in his hand. When he finally caught up with them he tried to talk, but instead he started to cry. Regaining his composure, he said, "I've been a waiter for many years, and this is the first time anybody has taken the time to tell me about the fine job I've been trying to do. I'll never forget tonight. And I'll always keep your notes. Thank you!"

The women in this story were compelled to give others what they had received. I believe it's almost impossible for you to make someone else feel better and not feel better yourself.

Tom Rath works with the Gallup Organization, known as one of the top polling institutions in the world. Over the course of fifty years Gallup surveyed more than four million employees on the topics of recognition and praise, and it discovered several key facts. First, regular recognition and praise increased employee productivity, built stronger teams, made for better safety records and fewer job-related accidents, and enhanced employee retention. Second, more than sixty-five percent of employees surveyed reported that they had received *no* recognition or praise at work in the previous year. It's no wonder that Rath reports the number-one reason people leave their jobs is a lack of appreciation.

In *How Full Is Your Bucket?* Tom Rath and Donald O. Clifton use a great metaphor to explain how appreciating others can make such a difference. Imagine that inside each of us is a bucket filled with positive emotions. Every time you say something nice to someone, when you praise or compliment or help someone out—anything to demonstrate caring and increase positive feelings—you are filling that person's bucket. However, any time you say or do things to decrease people's positive feelings, it's as if you were using a dipper to drain their buckets dry. When our emotional buckets are full, we feel we can accomplish anything. If our buckets are low or drained, we have no energy and lose our drive. At every moment we have a choice: to fill our own bucket or someone else's through positive thoughts, words, and deeds, or to be a drag and a drain on ourselves and others through negativity.

Will you be a bucket-filler or a bucket-dipper? What if you were to take any of these actions for friends or co-workers? How would these help to fill their buckets?

You could. . .

- Call someone to say "hi" and to see how he or she is doing.

- Encourage friends or co-workers to do their best.

- Stop to talk with people in your neighborhood or workplace.

- Help someone with an assignment or project.

- Say "good job" to someone after he or she has really worked hard.

- Cheer for a friend or colleague at a sports game, concert, play, or other performance.

- Talk with co-workers about their goals.

- Help someone work through a conflict.

There are two kinds of people in the world: those who pull you up and those who pull you down. When you notice the good things about others—*and tell them*—you become a pull-up person. Noticing and sincerely complimenting others has a tremendous influence on their productivity, their health—even their longevity. Make it a habit to say something positive to people on a daily basis.

CONNECTING THROUGH RESPECT

"I don't get no respect." When the late comedian Rodney Dangerfield uttered his trademark line, crowds roared with laughter. Maybe we laugh at Rodney Dangerfield's joke so we won't cry. We all desire to feel respected by others, but if truly we want respect, we must learn to give it first. Respect is the third feeling that's created when we notice what's needed and do our best to supply what's necessary.

Respecting others requires that you notice their needs. It doesn't necessarily mean you have to lie down and let them walk all over you, but it does mean you treat them with at least as much respect as you give yourself. How do you feel if others ignore you and show no regard for your needs? You might feel overlooked, unimportant—maybe even angry. However you might feel, it's not positive. Noticing is critical to showing others you care and building a mutual bond of respect and trust. Without that respect and trust, you won't truly connect.

U-TURN, Paul Manning's organization, builds self-respect through actions as well as words. While U-TURN was created to target low-income kids without financial means, the program is not free. Every kid who can afford it pays something, even if it's only a dollar a day. The kids with no money earn their way by washing dishes or doing some other chore. Paul refuses to create an environment that promotes dependency, which keeps people from moving to higher levels of living. By paying for the program, kids have a sense of ownership in the program and value in their contribution. They have self-respect.

DEMONSTRATE RESPECT THROUGH HIGH STANDARDS

By the time I was twelve years old, I was six feet, two inches tall. As a tall African-American kid growing up in Seattle I was expected by everybody to be great at basketball. But the only reason I ever got good at the game was my dad. He had done everything he could to encourage me to play basketball. He bought me my first new ball when I was in the third grade. When the regulation ten-foot-tall hoop was too high for me, he moved the hoop lower down so I could make more baskets. Every month or so he'd raise the hoop a little until I was making baskets consistently at the ten-foot height.

My dad respected me enough to hold me to incredibly high standards. At the time it didn't feel like respect, because he was very hard on me. I'd come home from a basketball game and tell my dad with pride how many points I'd scored. He'd usually say, "Remember, Keith, someone out there is working harder, and he's probably better than you. You'd better keep working hard if you want to be great."

All of us want praise from our fathers, and I'm no different. But in hindsight my dad gave me the gift of challenging me. He refused to let me use any standard other than being my best. When we played H.O.R.S.E. together, he cut me no slack and expected none. (H.O.R.S.E. is a version of basketball where two or more players shoot baskets, matching shot for shot. For example, if I shoot from the side and make a basket, you have to stand in exactly the same spot and make the same shot. Every time you're unable to make the same shot as the other player, you get a letter of the word HORSE. The first person to miss enough shots to spell out H.O.R.S.E. is the loser.) Because my dad respected me, I became a better player and a better man. Today I hold myself to high standards in every area of life because that's what my dad taught me.

Years ago someone told me that the three best words to motivate someone are "I love you," the four most motivating words are "I believe in you," and the five most motivating words are "I am proud of you." To me, offering someone respect encompasses all those words and then some. The right kind of respect combines both love and pride. It includes holding yourself and others to the highest standards because when you achieve those standards, you will feel you deserve respect.

NOTICING WHAT'S NEEDED ON A GLOBAL SCALE

In 2006 there were many well-known candidates for the Nobel Peace Prize: diplomats who had settled regional conflicts, NGOs (nongovernmental organizations) that were making a difference in Africa and Asia, men and women who had run monumental relief efforts following the 2004 tsunami. But the award went to someone unexpected: a Bangladeshi banker whose clients were the poorest of the poor.

Muhammad Yunus founded the Grameen Bank in 1976 with $27 of his own money. He wanted to make small loans to clients no other bank would consider—mostly women in rural Bangladesh. These women had no collateral and could barely feed their families. But Mr. Yunus felt that with a small amount of capital, these women could create businesses that would feed their families and lift them out of poverty forever.

The concept of microcredit proved incredibly workable. Women and men start small businesses doing everything from buying straw to make stools, to buying a cell phone and selling calling time to people in their villages, to making pickles or clothing or toys. Every week the lendees repay their loans a few dollars at a time. As of 2006 the Grameen bank had lent $5.72 billion to approximately 6.61 million borrowers at 2,226 branches. It has a ninety-eight percent repayment rate on its loans. Today, the concept of microcredit is used by banks in more than one hundred countries, giving people all over the world the chance to make their lives better through their own efforts.

Mr. Yunus is an exceptional example of this CONNECT step. He was aware of the enormous challenges faced by poor people all over the world. He noticed what was needed in his own country. He did what was necessary to offer people a way to increase their self-worth and self-respect. He cared enough for them not to offer a handout but instead to give them a way to lift themselves out of poverty.

As leaders, we know that our job is to be aware of others, notice their efforts, and do what's necessary to help them to seek the highest. We can care for them, respect their efforts, and urge them on to achieve more than they ever thought possible. When we do that, not only are we connecting with them, we are guiding them to become who they truly are. Always remember that self-worth, care, and respect begin with you and within you. When you have all three inside, you will naturally share these gifts with others.

NOTICE WHAT'S NEEDED AND DO WHAT'S NECESSARY ACTION STEPS

1. How will you notice what's needed among your friends, family, and co-workers? How will you do what's necessary to meet those needs? What can you be aware of that will help connect you more closely to others?

2. Like Ed Doherty, what can you do to create "wow" experiences for your employees, customers, communities, and suppliers? How can you go the extra mile to make people feel connected?

3. Has someone left you or left your workplace because you failed to notice their needs and do what was necessary to keep them in your life? What could you have done differently?

4. What are your unique gifts? What are you grateful for in your life? Make a list of all the things you value in your life, and spend a few moments giving thanks for all you have been given.

5. If negative experiences in your past have damaged your self-worth, remember that you can't change the past but you can always change your present and future. Do the exercise on pages 92–93 to list all the things you like about yourself. Read this list aloud to yourself at least once a day for a month.

6. How can you demonstrate caring for the people in your life? What can you do to care for your co-workers and customers? What small gestures would make the biggest difference?

7. Decide to write at least three people "I like you because . . ." notes each week. These can go to friends, family, co-workers, bosses, the cab driver who takes you to the airport, the newspaper carrier who puts your paper on the porch when it rains—anybody. Make your note short, uplifting, and specific. Hand it to the person with a smile, or leave it where you know he or she will find it. You will make someone's day a little better!

8. Commit to be a bucket-filler, not a bucket-dipper. Offer

positive words and deeds. Eliminate negativity in your own thoughts, words, and deeds, and do not accept it from anyone else. Don't let them steal your joy!

9. Respect yourself and others by acknowledging their greatness. Notice their needs and fill them.

10. Make sure that your respect includes holding yourself and others to high standards. This doesn't mean being harsh or cruel, but it does mean seeing their greatness and asking them to live up to who they truly are. Give them the support and encouragement they need to be their best!

11. Fill in the blank: **ICARE to be aware, notice what's needed, and do what's necessary in the following ways:**

_____.

CONNECT Step 4:
Navigate by Your Purpose

The purpose of life is a life of purpose.
—*Robert Byrne*

About fourteen years ago I was working for IBM as an instructor in marketing education, but I was getting ready to strike out on my own. I had created a small speaking business on the side. (I'd gotten a box of business cards from Office Depot, and I'd given two speeches for free.) As a trainer and speaker for IBM I felt that for the first time in my life I was doing what I was meant to do on this earth. I was making a difference in the lives of my co-workers and customers. But leaving the security of IBM was still a struggle. Like most people, I had doubts about my ability to make it on my own.

At that time a book came into my life: *Releasing Your Potential* by Dr. Myles Monroe. In it, Dr. Monroe wrote about finding the reason we were put on this earth. Each of us has a purpose and a vision; it's simply our job to find out that vision and purpose and fulfill both to the best of our ability. That message meant (and means) a lot to me because it really helped me keep focused on fulfilling my purpose.

Two weeks before I was to leave IBM, I found myself on a plane to Atlanta with Dr. Myles Monroe. I introduced myself, and we talked throughout the flight. I asked him several questions about my plan to start my own speaking business. Dr. Monroe reminded me of the need for focus and patience and said that I would soon lock into my purpose. "When you plant yourself in the ground like a seed, you're going to have to endure," he said. "Stay rooted like a seed in the ground in the calling and purpose for your life, and when you're planted, just like a seed one day you're going to sprout up and be able to make a difference in others by planting seeds in them."

When we arrived in Atlanta I walked Dr. Monroe to his gate, where we discovered his flight had been delayed two hours. "I believe this is a sign we should continue our conversation!" he told me with a smile. Then he invited me to attend a leadership conference he was holding in the Bahamas.

"Dr. Monroe, I'm all booked up that week," I said reluctantly. "The only day I'm available is Friday."

"That's the last day of the conference, and the day I'll be speaking," he replied.

"Then that's a sign—I'll be there," I told him.

Because of flight delays I made it to the conference that Friday five minutes after Dr. Monroe started speaking. After his talk, I ran into a friend of mine from Seattle. "Where have you been?" she asked. "The conference was incredible, but you missed most of it."

"What I received in the last two hours was worth the whole trip," I said jubilantly. Dr. Monroe's talk had confirmed for me that I was on the right track.

When I got back to Atlanta, I wrote Dr. Monroe to thank him for the conference and for his inspiration. Since he receives thousands of letters a week, I didn't really expect a reply. But four months later, I received a personal letter from Dr. Monroe. I had his letter framed, and today it hangs in my office at home.

Here's some of what Dr. Monroe wrote.

Dear Keith:

Warm greetings in Christ!

I wish to acknowledge receipt of your letter and deeply regret the delay in reply. This is due to my very hectic travel schedule and my desire to respond to you personally. I imagine you thought I had forgotten, but I assure you that our meeting was a point of destiny and our future is predestined to be together. I thank God for the opportunity to be a source of encouragement to you in some small way and I trust that you will continue to maximize your potential as you endeavor to fulfill God's purpose for your life.

Remember that within you lies a treasure that is yet to be uncovered and that anything you have done cannot be compared to what you are capable of doing. Never settle on your success but always strive to expose the hidden wealth that is left within. You are a great man and few people know it yet. I trust that you will die empty as you pour out of yourself all that God has given you birth for to deliver to this planet. You have my prayerful support in all that you do and if I can be of assistance to you in any of your endeavors or join you in any special seminar, please do not hesitate to contact me.

If we can be of any further help, please contact me and remember that eagles do not flock, they fly alone. May the spirit of the eagle be upon you.

Sincerely,

Your Brother and Friend in Christ

Dr. Myles E. Monroe

Dr. Monroe reminded me of the truth we all hold inside: that we were put on this earth for a reason and a purpose. As we said in an earlier chapter, you have unique gifts within you. Your purpose involves expressing those gifts. An old proverb says, "A man's gifts will make room for him." When you discover your

> **Purpose is nothing without action. And action requires vision.**

gifts and align your purpose with their expression, the world opens before you. The fourth CON-NECT principle is to *navigate by your purpose.*

A sense of purpose is not enough, however. You can feel you have a purpose to help cure disease, but if all you do is feel, that won't get you very far. Purpose is nothing without action. And action requires vision. We must create a clear vision of how our purpose can be accomplished on earth. We need the third BE-Attitude: *be vision centered.* Vision connects our purpose and gifts. When we connect with our purpose and vision, not only can we lead ourselves in creating great things, but also we can lead others.

LIVING WITH PURPOSE

Some people know their purpose very early in life. Great artists like Michelangelo and Leonardo da Vinci started drawing and studying art when they were very young. Mozart was composing music when he was four years old. Dr. Monroe wrote the purpose and vision for his life when he was thirteen. Many of us, however, have to wander through the wilderness a little before we discover why we were put on earth. Perhaps we need to find and develop our gifts.

I did a lot of searching of my own soul through the years to discover my purpose. I thought for a while that my purpose would involve being a professional basketball player. Then I thought it would be found in my work at IBM. But all the while, the experiences of my life were leading me to discover my real mission and purpose for being on earth: to motivate people and share with them the good news that they are great and capable of great things. Once this purpose became clear to me, I could create a vision for my life that has led me to where I am today.

You too have a grand purpose—a reason for your life. You may already know what it is, or you may have a vague sense of it within you. Or perhaps you are wandering through the wilderness, searching for your reason for being on this earth. If you do nothing else, take the time to do whatever it takes to connect to your sense of purpose.

For many of you this involves looking back at your life. When have you felt as if you were using your gifts to their fullest? When do you feel you have made the biggest difference in your own life or the lives of others? If you could do anything in the world, what would give you the greatest sense of accomplishment and fulfillment? Most often our purpose is tied to our deepest desires. What is something you would like to do with your life but you've never dared even to state it?

Now, your purpose doesn't have to be earth shattering. Your purpose can be to nurture your children or grandchildren. Your purpose can be to create a beautiful garden. Your purpose can be to be an incredible teammate, or an amazing husband or wife, or an inspiring teacher, or someone who consoles the bereaved. Your purpose in life may be to be a role model of someone who endures great affliction and still uplifts others. Your purpose could be to provide for your family and be a pillar of your community. There are as many purposes as there are people on earth. In the same way each person is a unique soul, we are each created with a unique purpose.

Your purpose may or may not gain you great wealth or fame, but when you discover your purpose and use it to guide your life, you'll feel connected in a way that you could never have imagined. You'll be using the gifts given to you, and you'll be walking the path mapped out for your success.

VISION IS THE ROAD MAP OF PURPOSE

In 1776, delegates from thirteen colonies along the eastern coast of North America gathered in Philadelphia, Pennsylvania. These men had experienced growing frustration with what they saw as oppressive laws and actions by the British government. They felt strongly that the colonies in America deserved to govern themselves. They came together with the purpose of making that happen by either peaceable means or open rebellion.

But they needed something that would make the British government understand this purpose and what the colonists planned. So the delegates asked Thomas Jefferson to write a document that would articulate both the colonists' grievances and what they proposed for the future.

The document Thomas Jefferson created was the Declaration of Independence—a vision that would form the foundation of the United States of America. When the delegates read Jefferson's words, they were inspired to take action. The Declaration was signed in July 1776. In many ways, the vision it describes is still the driving force of the spirit of the United States of America.

Vision is the road map for our purpose. It takes our deepest desires and lays them out for the entire world to see. Vision connects our purpose to our actions. Purpose gets us up in the morning, but vision tells us what to do once we're out of bed. If purpose is the still small voice inside us that pushes us to set our feet on the path for our lives, vision shows us the prize at the end of the road and how to get from where we are to where we need to be.

In *The Principles and Power of Vision*, Dr. Monroe writes, "Sight is a function of the eyes, but vision is a function of the heart." Vision is born in the heart. It pulses through you and sustains your life. When we don't have a vision, we lose our passion. One of my favorite sayings is this: "Without a vision, people perish." We all need something to live for and to work toward. Vision shows us what our lives will be like when we reach the goals we set for ourselves. It keeps us going when things are tough because we know the prize is worth the effort. When we center ourselves on a vision that truly comes from the heart, one that fulfills our purpose and allows us to use our gifts, then we can steer our life by that vision with confidence in our eventual success.

DEFINE YOUR VISION

Having defined and possibly refined your purpose earlier in this chapter, you now can start to envision how that purpose will play out in your life. What's your vision for yourself? Vision is how you see yourself today, tomorrow, next week, next year, in five years, and so on. Let your imagination soar. Dare to dream. Visualize yourself doing the things you want to do or living the way you want to live. Do you want to lose weight? See yourself as thin. Do you want to win your company's sales award and incentive trip to Hawaii? See yourself on the beach, soaking up the tropical sun. Do you want to head up a company? See yourself sitting in the executive suite with "CEO" engraved on your office door. Do you want reconciliation with a family member? See yourself embracing that person.

Don't worry if your vision doesn't reflect your current reality. Dr. Monroe tells us, "Vision is seeing the future before it comes into being. It is a mental picture of your destiny. . . . Only by seeing what is not yet here can you bring something new, creative, and exciting into existence."

I believe there are four secrets for creating a vision to steer your life.

> Vision is seeing the future before it comes into being.
> —Dr. Myles E. Monroe

1. Make your vision vivid

Fred and Harry were two old men who shared a room in a nursing home. Fred had the bed by the window, and every morning he would regale Harry with stories of what he saw outside. "There's a parade this morning!" he'd say one day. The next he would declare, "I can see a bunch of kids playing tag in the park. They're running around like crazy—boy, do they look like they're having fun." Another day he'd report, "We had snow last night. Everything's covered with a beautiful coat of white. The tree branches are laden with it. There's a big dog running through the snow. It's so cold out I can see its breath from here." Fred told Harry all about the life he could see from the window, and Harry loved every minute of it.

After about a year, Fred died. Harry sorely missed his friend and thought, "It sure would be nice to see what Fred was describing all these years. It'd feel like he was still here." So he asked one of the nurses if he could move to the bed by the window. The staff moved him one evening when it was dark outside.

In the morning Harry awoke with great anticipation. Now he'd be able to see for himself everything Fred had been talking about! He opened his eyes and turned to look out the window—and his jaw dropped. He pushed the call button and a nurse bustled in.

"What happened to the view? All I can see out this window is a brick wall. Where's the park? Where are the trees that Fred told me about?"

The nurse smiled at Harry. "That window's always faced the wall of the other wing of the hospital. But it didn't matter, because Fred was blind."

Vision uses the eyes of the heart to create pictures for our eyes and mind. To have a vision that will keep you going no matter what, those pictures must be so vivid, specific, exciting, and compelling that we will do what it takes to make them real. When you describe your vision, use all your senses. Make it something that will cause you to get out of bed early in the morning and stay up late at night.

2. Be clear about exactly what your vision will give you and what it will require of you

Throughout high school and college, I played basketball. For most of that time I had a vision of eventually playing professional basketball in the NBA, specifically for my hometown team, the Seattle Supersonics. But the first year I was eligible for the NBA draft, the Supersonics were NBA champs and drafted only two players. What's more, the competition that year included Larry Bird and Magic Johnson. Needless to say, things were tough, and I didn't get the call. But later that summer I was recruited by a professional basketball team in Rotterdam, Holland.

I thought about the offer for twenty-four hours; then I called the coach back and said no. I felt I had developed my gifts playing basketball, but continuing to chase my dream of a pro career in Europe didn't really fit my vision for what I wanted to do with my life. Basketball had given me a chance to work hard, dedicate myself to a goal, and come out a winner through my own efforts. All those traits could be used in arenas other than sports. That's when I made the decision to go into business and applied to work for the company I considered the best in the world at the time: IBM.

Sometimes it's easy to confuse a vision of what we want in life with the means that will get us there. We can accomplish a vision in many different ways. I know men and women whose vision includes being parents, but for reasons beyond their control they never have biological children. Does that mean they cannot fulfill their vision? Of course not. They can adopt children or be foster parents. They could choose a career that focuses on children, such as teaching or day care. They might work with kids in after-school activities, or mentor young people in job training programs. They might become health care providers and nurture children who are sick. All these means will fulfill the vision of nurturing young lives.

You also must be clear on what your vision will require of you. Will you need to add skills, training, or education? What relationships will you need to develop as part of your vision? Few of us accomplish the vision for our lives alone; who needs to be enrolled with you in the excitement and passion of your vision?

I believe that we're all given a purpose in life and the vision to make that purpose real. I also believe that our vision must be big enough to encompass all the wonderful gifts that come our way. If you focus clearly on your purpose, you can adapt your vision to fit the circumstances needed for your success.

3. Make sure your vision causes you to grow

Your vision for yourself should be something that causes you to stretch and grow. Indeed, I've found that often when I feel the most nervous about an opportunity, that's a sure sign that I need to expand and grow my vision of what's possible.

One Friday when I was working at IBM, I got a call from the company HR department. The woman on the other line was distressed. "Keith, I need someone to speak for forty minutes at a career day for five hundred minority high school seniors. I know it's short notice, but I'm in a real bind. Can you do it?"

"What should I talk about?" I asked her.

"Anything you like—you'll be sharing the stage with judges, attorneys, doctors, and top businesspeople from the community."

I agreed to do it, but as soon as I put the phone down I started to get stressed. What would I have to say compared with all the high-powered professionals on the panel? At 7 AM the next morning I called my best friend, Ralph.

"What in the world can I talk to these kids about?" I asked him.

"Talk to them about attitude and winning the game of life," he said. "Tell them about playing basketball and how you had to sit out a year and the NBA draft and getting hired at IBM. You're always saying that attitude is everything—talk about that."

I calmed down after talking to Ralph. When I went to the auditorium and spoke that day, I received a standing ovation. It was the very first time I delivered my message about the importance of keeping a positive attitude in life, and it launched my career as a motivational speaker. That day changed my vision for my life forever. It caused me to adopt a vision that was so much greater than any I had had before.

Your vision not only should feel exciting and compelling—it also should make you a little uncomfortable because it's bigger than where you currently are in your life. Only when your vision compels you to grow will it truly fulfill the purpose of your life.

4. Connect your vision to a greater good

Who besides you will benefit from your vision? For it to be truly compelling, you must connect your vision to something bigger than yourself. Dr. Monroe writes, "True vision is unselfish. . . . [It] should always focus on helping humanity or building up others in some way." We aren't put on earth just so we can earn a living, buy more toys, and eat more food. Everything we do affects other people for good or evil. When we create a vision for our lives, it's our responsibility to take the good of others into account.

This doesn't mean your vision can't include doing well! I

believe that when we follow our vision and live according to our purpose, then we'll receive what we need to achieve both. While we certainly have to put in the effort on our side, I believe that when we follow our vision and purpose, we will be provided for abundantly.

PURPOSE, VISION, ACTION

Knowing what you want to do and why—for whom and for what purpose—is the first step toward fulfilling your vision. Unfortunately, some people stop there. They never take action to make their vision a reality. But vision without action is nothing but a pipe dream. Vision without action is like a mirage in the desert: all it does is pull us off course and leave us stumbling and gasping for water.

Living out your purpose and putting your vision into action is not for the fainthearted. It takes hard work. It takes mapping out a plan of action—creating a strategic to-do list with carefully determined steps. Action makes vision practical and real.

Achieving a vision is like climbing a set of stairs. There are steps that we must take to reach the reward awaiting us at the top. The vision has different levels that we must climb and conquer. Each step upward is a small piece of our vision brought down to the practical. We also call these pieces of our vision *goals.*

Imagine that you've never been a runner and one day you decide you'd like to participate in a marathon. You have a vision of crossing the finish line in triumph, proud of having accomplished a significant physical feat of endurance. But to attain that vision, you have to take a lot of steps (literally and figuratively) between now and your triumphant

Vision without action is nothing but a pipe dream.

finish. You need to set a series of interim goals so you'll be ready to run more than 26 miles when the time comes. Your first goal might be to jog a half a mile. Once you've done that for a week, you'll set a goal of a mile, then 2, then 3. Eventually it will be 15, then 20, and finally 26.2 miles. Your goals will continue to grow and expand to fit your vision of running your first marathon successfully.

Goals make our visions attainable. They help make even the biggest visions practical. A salesperson might be overwhelmed when she looks at the target of a six-figure sales quota, for example. But a goal of closing three sales a week, while ambitious, may challenge rather than overwhelm her. And those three sales a week, added together, will produce the bottom line the company is asking for.

Once you have a goal, you can break it down into the specific actions needed to accomplish it. That salesperson with the quota may need to make thirty more calls a week to close those three sales. That breaks down to six more calls a day—a very specific action. Or perhaps you have a vision of creating a strong and supportive environment for your family. Your goal is for the family to spend quality time together on a regular basis. Your action this week is to cook a great meal that you know your family will love sharing. Keeping your goal and vision in mind as you prepare dinner will make the work all the more enjoyable.

THE POWER OF TEAM VISION AND PURPOSE

The only things that can create a team and hold it together are vision and purpose. The company you work for has a vision or mission statement. Maybe you are involved in a community service group, or the PTA, or your son's soccer team, and each of those organizations has a vision. You might have a vision of what you want your family to be. We all have individual visions, whether they relate to personal or professional aspirations. You are also called upon to work alongside others to accomplish the visions for your team, your church group, your association, or your business. But without a vision and purpose, your team, group, association, or business is less likely to succeed.

Vision provides the inspiration that creates perspiration. It makes us work harder as a team than we will ever work on our own. The great business management expert Peter Drucker said, "People work for a cause, not just for a living." There is something about belonging to a group with shared vision and shared values that inspires greatness. A shared purpose and vision that generate passion are the surest connective "glue" your team and business can have. If you want to build success through people and performance, your vision and your purpose had better be strong.

When you are a member of a team, how you fulfill your role will help determine the success or failure of the team vision. Nowhere is that clearer than in sports. The goals of a sports team are tangible, the steps taken to reach them are practical, and the passion with which coaches and players execute those goals is fervent. We can all learn from what transpires on and off the field when a team is trying to win a game and ultimately a championship.

When actually playing on a team, each player has a vision that is tied to his position. In football, every player has his individual assignment, but all eleven players on the offense must work together to execute a play that will fulfill the vision of scoring a touchdown. The same goes for the eleven defensive players, who must work together to accomplish the vision of stopping the opponent from advancing. The entire team is working toward the ultimate vision of winning the game. When all the players/team members, associates, or employees in an organization know their individual assignments while also understanding the organization's shared vision and purpose, they will execute what they have to do individually and work together as a team. And when teams work together toward their shared vision and purpose, attaining goals becomes far easier, and success is assured.

LEADERS COMMUNICATE AN INSPIRING VISION

The first job of a coach, team leader, CEO, or manager at work is to inspire his or her team with a powerful vision and a common purpose. You met Go Roma Italian Kitchen restaurant developer Yorgo Koutsogiorgas earlier in this book. Yorgo is a master of conveying purpose and vision to his employees and getting them to work together toward common goals. He inspires dishwashers and restaurant managers alike to buy into the company's vision for success by instilling in them a belief that they are an integral part of a purpose bigger than themselves. He tells new employees, "It's up to you whether your view your work as trivial or consider it to be the most important endeavor that ever existed."

Yorgo illustrates the point with a familiar story about a group of bricklayers working at a construction site. When a man approached one of the bricklayers and asked him what he was doing, the bricklayer looked up and said in an annoyed voice, "Can't you see? I'm laying bricks for a wall."

The man apologized for bothering him and moved on. He came across a second bricklayer several yards away and asked him the same question. The bricklayer looked up with pride and said, "Can't you see? I'm part of a team that is building a magnificent cathedral!"

Yorgo uses this story to convey to his employees that even the busboy who picks up dirty dishes plays an important role in satisfying customers and making Go Roma Italian Kitchen a first-class restaurant. If Yorgo encounters an unhappy customer, he takes full responsibility and finds a solution to the problem. However, when a customer is eager to compliment someone,

Yorgo gets an employee from the kitchen or from the floor and brings him to the table to hear what the customer has to say. The employee becomes the recipient of the compliment, even if the comment the customer has to make does not directly relate to that employee's work, because the employee has played a part in that customer's positive experience. When the employee understands that his role is critical to the restaurant's vision and purpose, he has renewed passion and zeal for both.

LEARNING TO COACH OTHERS

As a leader you must keep your team inspired by purpose and vision for the long term. That means you must be not only a leader but a coach. Leaders communicate purpose and vision, but coaches show us how we can turn vision into reality. A great coach leads from the front, from the rear, from the side—wherever he or she can best serve the players and the vision.

Great coaches help us keep going to achieve even the most out-of-reach vision. One of the greatest coaches I've ever seen was Ray Pelletier. Ray was known as America's business attitude coach, but he also helped to turn around many prominent sports teams. About ten years ago, I got a call from a client who was a big booster of North Carolina State's football team. "Keith, the team was 3–8 last year and they need some help with their attitude," he said. "Can you come and speak with them?"

"Sure, but I'm not the guy you want," I told him. "You want my mentor, Coach Pelletier. He's the best at coaching teams to find the best inside themselves. Let me call him for you."

Coach Pelletier agreed to take on the team, but only if I came along with him. "Keith, I'm an out-of-shape white guy who never played any sport seriously," he said. "You were a super athlete and you understand what these guys are going through. You need to be doing what I'm doing, so come and learn."

I'll always remember that training with the NC State Wolfpack football team. Coach Pelletier started the session by saying, "Look, I don't know anything about football. I don't understand all the X's and O's and the plays you make on the field. But I do know about getting people to achieve more than they ever thought possible. And it starts by each of you answering one important question: Are you coachable? Because if so, let's roll up our sleeves and get to work."

NC State's opening game of the season was against Syracuse University, a team that was ranked thirteenth in national college football. Coach Pelletier helped the entire NC State team leave behind its losing mentality. "The big orange S in the middle of the field stands for State, not Syracuse," he told them. "When you walk on that field, you must say to yourselves, 'This is our house. We own it.'"

Coach Pelletier also reminded the players of the power of team. He had each young man put a rubber band around his wrist. "You all know how easy it is to break one rubber band," he said. "But put three, four, ten rubber bands together and what happens? The strongest man on earth can't break them. Your greatest strength lies in this team and working together to achieve victory."

NC State went into the game with Syracuse 25-point underdogs. They won the game by one point in overtime with a two-point conversion after a touchdown. The team acknowledged the power of Ray Pelletier's inspirational coaching by giving him the game ball.

Whether in sports, at home, or in business, part of a coach's job is to create the vision and then get others to believe that vision is possible. For example, at Verizon Wireless, Jim McGean helps sales people of an entire region navigate toward a common vision of reaching what he calls competitive greatness. But Jim's coaching skills were honed years earlier when he was in graduate school and he coached a college baseball team at Emory University in Atlanta.

Officially the team was only a baseball club, but Jim's vision was to raise the team to varsity status. He wanted the baseball program to eventually become one of the best in the country. He didn't let the fact that they had no field and no money get in the way of his resolve. Instead, he set out to coach others into catching his vision.

First, Jim had to convince other college varsity teams to play Emory. That was a job in and of itself. From a varsity team's perspective, playing a "club team" was a wasted day because the game wouldn't count. But the Emory club wouldn't be certified for varsity play unless it started acting like a varsity team. When the other coaches understood Jim's vision, they were happy to be part of the solution and agreed to have their Division 1, 2, or 3 teams play against Emory.

Surprisingly, it was a greater challenge to inspire the Emory baseball team members! Jim had to connect to the players, listening and learning so he could discover what motivated each of them. Some wanted a team as good as or better than any varsity program at the school. Others just wanted to play baseball. By understanding the level of passion and commitment of each player, Jim got the buy-in he needed. He raised the team to varsity status. Two decades later, the Emory University Eagles are one of the top ten Division 3 baseball teams in the country.

Great coaches are great listeners. They're also willing to let their players shine while they lead from the sidelines. More important, they're dedicated to doing whatever it takes to help the team grow as together they pursue a common vision and purpose. When you are a great coach and leader, your team will run off the field saying, "We did it!" not "Coach did it." And you'll have the enormous satisfaction of having helped an entire team fulfill its vision and purpose along with your own.

> **Great coaches are great listeners.**

HOW TO MAKE YOUR VISION
AND PURPOSE A REALITY

When you and your team possess a strong vision and purpose, you will run out onto the field of life ready to play and to give your all in pursuit of your goals. Sometimes you'll cruise down the field and score easily. But more often the game will be hard fought and will take all your energy and resources. In some ways, that's good, because the best way for us to learn and grow is to strive against a worthy opponent. If David hadn't come face to face with Goliath, he'd probably have ended his days as a shepherd somewhere in the middle of Judea. But when we pursue our vision and purpose, usually we will have to use all of ourselves and then some to achieve success.

I believe there are five secrets of turning vision and purpose into reality.

1. Follow a winning plan

When you come up with your goals and actions, you may find that you need to add resources or skills to accomplish them. After all, goals and visions are designed to stretch us beyond our current capacity, so it's possible that you'll need some help. Very few of us do things alone, thank goodness. We don't have to invent the wheel every time we want to take a trip to the grocery store. We don't have to figure out how an internal combustion engine works in order to start the car. And we don't have to figure out each and every step we will need to take to achieve our visions and goals, because there are so many great examples and role models who have gone before us in this world.

Let's go back to that vision of running a marathon. You can create your own goals and action plan for accomplishing your vision—but what if you had a coach to help you? What if you had a training buddy who'd run several marathons before and was willing to work with you as you prepared for the race?

I believe in learning from the best and getting the best coaching possible when it comes to pursuing the vision for my life. Sometimes the coaching comes from my pastor, other performance coaches, friends, family, co-workers, bosses, teachers, or mentors. Some of the best coaches I've encountered deliver their material in the form of books, seminars, and courses. I use what I learn for practical advice on how to live and how to accomplish my goals.

When you are working toward a specific goal, I suggest you create your own playbook by gathering wisdom from trusted sources and from people who have already successfully navigated the path you are on. There is nothing new on the face of the earth. Something has been written about whatever it is you are trying to accomplish. Follow strategies that have worked for others, customizing them to your specific circumstances. Connect with people who are where you want to be. Study under them. Learn from the best. And remember that your best guidance often comes from keeping firmly connected to your purpose.

2. Put on the uniform every day

Imagine that attaining your vision is like playing in a football game. You know that your ultimate vision is to be victorious at the end of four quarters. You will have plays and drives—goals—to accomplish so that you can attain your vision. It's hoped that you've had great coaching and you've studied your playbook, so you know what to do. The last thing you must do before you go out onto the field is to "suit up." You must put on certain protective pieces of clothing so you can play hard, take hits during the game, and still be victorious.

In life you must put on different kinds of protective "equipment" to ensure that you will stay strong no matter what the challenges. Every day you must wear the helmet of a new and positive mind-set. Just as a coach gives the team a pep talk before going out on the field, you need to give yourself a pregame speech before you go out in life. Focus on the reasons why you can fulfill your purpose, and then put on the helmet to protect your mind from the negative influences around you. You have control over what goes into your mind. You have chosen to read this book, for example. You can choose which voices you listen to in your life and keep only the ones that offer constructive input. Notice I didn't say "only positive input." Sometimes we need to listen to things that may seem negative in the moment but are designed to help us become better and keep us on track. However, you are in charge of what input you allow and what you do with the input you receive. You always have a choice to create positive, constructive meanings from the experiences and advice life offers you.

After you put on the uniform of your purpose and the helmet of the right mind-set, you must put on the mouthguard of the right words. The words you speak—whether positive or negative—have a way of rooting themselves in your psyche and coming to pass. Not only do your words affect you, they have a positive or negative influence on others. Don't let negative words derail your vision. Speak in the positive to yourself and others.

Next are the shoulder pads of internal strength of mind and heart. This will protect you from the onslaught of negative circumstances. Shoulder pads extend over your chest. When you put on shoulder pads, you are protecting your heart, which is where your vision is born. Protect your vision.

Finally, put on the cleats of your core values so you can keep your footing. Stay rooted and grounded in your core values and in the reasons you decided to pursue your vision in the first place.

3. Turn your "have-to's" into "want-to's"

If you want to fulfill your vision, you must discipline yourself to do what it takes. You must create a regimen that will lead you to your vision for your life. My pastor, Dr. Creflo A. Dollar of World Changers Church International, says that a regimen consists of the things you do every day whether you feel like doing them or not. Discipline occurs when you make a mental decision to do the things you *have* to do—even if they're not what you *want* to do.

A lot of kids might say they want to be like basketball star Kobe Bryant of the Los Angeles Lakers. But are those kids prepared to get up at 4:00 every morning and shoot the number of jump shots he does? Are they willing to sacrifice the hours and hours he works to be one of the best in the NBA? Those are the have-to's for anyone even hoping to play at the professional level. If you are going to acquire the discipline to accomplish both personal and professional success, your "have-to's" must become your "want-to's."

It's not easy. You will have to postpone today's pleasures for tomorrow's vision. But if you persist, your results will reflect your decision. One day you will realize that your regimen has become a discipline. It's automatic. That's when you will truly tap into your potential and turn your vision into reality.

4. Build up a strong and flexible defense

So you create a vision and the goals to attain it. You acquire the skills and elicit the help you need to execute successfully. You put on your uniform so you can play well for the full game. You develop a regimen, which becomes a discipline. You build a strong offense, and you're putting points on the board. You seem to be moving quickly toward attaining your vision. Then suddenly, out of nowhere, a pass is intercepted or you fumble the ball. It is now time for your defense to take the field.

There are times when life will score against you and you will need a strong defense to fight the challenges that come your way. Defense helps you with a down economy. Defense helps you deal with a job loss. Defense helps you when illness strikes or a hurricane ravages your home or a relationship is broken. Defense helps you block and tackle against the negativity that will attempt to invade your mind and heart.

Your defense had better be flexible, because you don't know what life is going to throw at you. Life's like that: you're following your game plan, and then people, places, and circumstances over which you have no control throw your game off. You'd better be able to adapt. You might need to take a different path to your vision.

On the other hand, changes in your external environment may cause you to rethink your vision. Market changes might cause a company to reinvent itself to meet evolving customer needs. A vision must remain fluid and flexible to some extent to allow for growth, change, and opportunity.

Remember Southwest Airlines? Southwest was a small regional carrier when a team of executives got together and started to rethink their vision and purpose. Instead of trying to compete with the big airlines, Southwest decided to become the mass transit of the air. Southwest radically revised (or re-envisioned) what an airline should be. The airlines put fun and on-time performance first rather than luxury. Southwest standardized its airplanes, maintenance, training—everything possible—while allowing the flight attendants to express their individuality through jokes and lighthearted banter with passengers. As Southwest has grown into one of the big airlines it has continued to re-envision itself while staying true to its purpose of providing low-cost air travel to the largest possible number of people.

5. Never give up, cave in, or quit

You may get behind in the game, and it may look as if you don't have a chance to win. But it's not over till it's over. Even if you lose a game or two, it's still not over. It's only over when you quit.

Quitting isn't part of Bobby Martin's vocabulary. During his senior year at Colonel White High in Dayton, Ohio, Bobby was the most popular student in school. He played nose tackle for the junior varsity and varsity football teams. His plans were to go to college and then pursue a career in computer software design. Sounds like thousands of kids in small towns across America—but Bobby Martin was born without legs.

For as long as Bobby could remember, his mother had taught him to be independent. There was no room for self-pity. Bobby loved sports, so, with a coach's encouragement, he tried out for and made his middle school wrestling team. And he was good! As an eighth grader he took second place in the city-wide tournament.

Wrestling is one thing, but how in the world could anyone play football with no legs? Players run hundreds of yards in each game. It's a high-impact sport and very rough. But Bobby was not deterred. In his day-to-day life, he uses his arms to walk when he's not zipping around on a skateboard. He told the coaches he would walk with his arms on the football field. But Bobby did more than walk. His vision was to be a nose tackle, and he made it happen. Bobby was a success on the football field, contributing to the success of the team. More important, he is a success off the field, motivating everyone he comes in contact with.

When you connect to your own vision and purpose, you'll discover a drive and power that you never would have thought possible. And when you share a vision and purpose with your team, your company, or your family, you will be connected at the deepest level, and together there will be no mountain you can't climb.

VISION AND PURPOSE PULL YOU THROUGH

One of my favorite stories of the power of purpose is found in the life of Navy Master Diver Carl Brashear. The son of sharecroppers in rural Kentucky, Carl left school after the seventh grade. At seventeen he joined the U.S. Navy. Carl had a vision and purpose for his life: he wanted to be a Navy diver. He put up with enormous discrimination because of his race, but finally he was allowed to attend diving school and qualify as a diver.

Carl had fulfilled his vision for his life—but his greatest test was yet to come. In the 1960s he was part of a salvage team that was sent to recover a nuclear bomb that had been lost off the coast of Spain. He was helping to bring a small boat alongside the Navy vessel when the boat broke loose and toppled onto the deck. Carl pushed several sailors out of the way, but the boat knocked loose a mooring pipe that hit Carl's leg, breaking it in several places.

The doctors told Carl they could piece his leg back together, but it would take him three years to recover, and the leg would always be three inches shorter than the other one. "I can't stay in the hospital that long—I've got to go back to diving!" Carl told them. He insisted that the doctors amputate his leg. And that's when Carl's real journey began.

Carl was determined to return to diving for the Navy. When

he received his prosthetic leg, he left his crutches at the prosthetic center and walked out of the door on his new leg, and he never used crutches again. He created a physical training program to get his strength back. He applied to go back through diving school to prove his fitness. Even though he was at least two decades older than most of the other students, Carl led the other recruits in calisthenics and runs every day. Some days he'd come back from those runs with a puddle of blood in the top of his artificial leg—he had rubbed his stump raw. But he'd just soak the leg in a bucket of hot water and salt, and get up the next morning and run again. The young recruits didn't even know that Carl was an amputee until he went into the swimming pool with them and came out with his prosthetic leg tucked under his arm! At the end of a year, Carl Brashear was restored to active duty as a Navy diver, the first amputee ever to do so. He retired from the Navy after thirty years of service.

Carl Brashear had an incredibly strong vision and purpose for his life. He would not let anything—lack of education, racial discrimination, a devastating physical injury, even the might and power of the U.S. Navy—stand in the way of his dream. He was lifted up above other men because of his faith in himself and his path. And his story inspires men and women everywhere to hold to their own purpose and vision, no matter what.

NAVIGATE BY YOUR PURPOSE ACTION STEPS

1. What is your purpose in life? You may know it already, or you may need to discover it within yourself. What is the reason you were put here on earth?

2. Once you know your purpose, you can create a vision for how that purpose will manifest. What's your vision for how you want your life to be? Do you see yourself helping children? Leading a team at work and making a differ-

ence? Being part of an incredible family? Describe your vision in specific, exciting, and compelling terms. Make sure you know exactly what that vision will give you and what it will require of you. Make sure your vision is one that will cause you to grow and that connects you to a greater good.

3. Purpose and vision without action are worth very little. What's your action plan? Outline a plan with strategic steps that will help you achieve your vision.

4. Do you have a clear vision and purpose for your family and your teams at work? If you lead a team, have you communicated the vision clearly to the team members? Are they enthusiastically enrolled in accomplishing that vision? Does each team member understand the role he or she plays in helping the team to achieve its goals?

5. As a leader, are you also a great coach? Do you lead from the front or from the sidelines? Does your team say "We did it!" when goals are accomplished, feeling as if they have all done it as a group?

6. Remember the five secrets of turning your vision and purpose into reality. How are you using them in your life?

   • What's your playbook? Do you have a winning game plan?

   • Do you get ready each day by putting on the helmet of a positive mind-set, the mouth guard of the right words, the shoulder pads of internal strength of mind and heart, and the cleats of your core values?

   • Are you developing discipline by creating a regimen of things you have to do in order to succeed? How will you turn your have-to's into want-to's?

- What is your strong and flexible defense? How are you adjusting your vision to suit changing conditions while still keeping your eye on the goal?

- Like Bobby Martin, are you committed to never give up, cave in, or quit until you achieve your vision and purpose?

7. Fill in the blank: **ICARE to take action now by doing**

_____

to live according to my purpose and vision.

CONNECT Step 5:

Execute Ethically:
Do What's Right
Because It's Right

Practice what you want to become.
—*Dr. Creflo A. Dollar*

Located in the blue-collar community of Richmond, California, on the east side of San Francisco Bay, Richmond High School has always been a tough place to go to school. Gangs and drugs were common on the streets of the town, and academics were a low priority. The school was poorly equipped and often dangerous. One of the few bright spots at Richmond High was the school's basketball team. At the start of the year, the team was undefeated, with a record of 13–0. Varsity basketball players were treated like the stars of the school.

However, their coach, Ken Carter, was less than pleased. At the beginning of the season he had had every player sign an academic contract in which the player agreed to maintain a 2.3 average, stay off the streets, attend all classes, and sit in the front row. In class the players were supposed to participate in discussions and to complete and turn in all their homework on time. Some of the kids kept their word, but others were struggling. Fifteen of forty-five players had started to skip classes. Carter had these young men doing push-ups and running laps to teach them the consequences of their actions, but to little effect. So Carter decided to take a more drastic course.

One day before school opened, the young men on the basketball team arrived for their regular practice only to find the gym doors chained and padlocked. On the door was a note from Coach Carter: "NO PRACTICE TODAY—All basketball players report to the library." Carter had suspended the school's basketball program—freshman, junior varsity, and varsity—until the team got its academic life in order. The time usually allocated for basketball practice would be used for study, supervised by teachers and tutors.

The reaction to Carter's decision was swift and negative. Parents and school officials vilified him for benching the school's first undefeated team and losing a chance to win the state championship. But Carter held firm. He'd seen too many former high school basketball stars on the streets of Richmond—young men who had neglected their education and now were criminals or in gangs or simply unemployed and poor. "You'll play basketball for a few years if you're lucky. But your education you're going to use a lifetime," Carter told the players.

After the team had forfeited two games, the teachers reported that the players' academics were improving, so Coach Carter ended the lockout. The team went 19–5 that season and made it to the district playoffs. But Carter's real won-loss record was a clean sweep—*every member of that year's varsity team finished high school and went on to some form of higher education.*

Ken Carter could have let his basketball players continue their unbeaten season. He could have made excuses or focused on the players who were doing well academically and written off the others as lost causes. Instead, Coach Carter did what he believed was the ethical thing to do in the circumstances. His actions made him very unpopular in the short term, but the results of his actions proved he was right.

To connect with yourself and other people is not a squishy, touchy-feely kind of thing because at its core, you must connect with the highest and best in yourself and others. You also must connect firmly with what is right in any given situation. Even when it's not easy or when taking the high road will cause you pain, you must make the ethical choice if you are going to maintain the most important connections of all: with your conscience and your Creator. The fifth CONNECT principle is *execute ethically: do what's right because it's right*.

THE COST OF SACRIFICING
INTEGRITY FOR PERFORMANCE

The BE-Attitude for this step is to *be performance and integrity driven*. I believe you need to have both performance *and* integrity to succeed in the long term. Unfortunately, integrity is usually the first thing thrown overboard whenever a company's performance is below par. Businesses are under constant pressure to exceed revenue and profit forecasts so they can keep their stock prices rising. It is very easy to make up a plan that isn't ethical, that doesn't have integrity, that doesn't do something the right way in order to hit a short-term goal. Rather than focusing on performance with integrity, many businesses focus on performance at any cost.

But in the long run, while results are important, *how* you reach those results is what really matters. If you forfeit integrity to get what you want, the results are meaningless because they will not last. Remember the former executive leaders of Enron, Tyco, and WorldCom? There was a time when they had the world by the tail. In reality, the success they built for themselves crumbled because it was built on a foundation of corruption.

> People who make unethical choices may succeed for a moment, but ultimately they pay a price.

And it's not just business that seems to sacrifice integrity on the altar of performance. Look at any number of politicians who have stepped down in disgrace. The power they wielded turned to humiliation when scandals revealed unethical or illegal behavior. Look at many top athletes. The use of steroids has become so prevalent that the United States Congress held hearings on the use of performance-enhancing drugs in major league baseball. Olympic athletes have had their medals stripped when it was learned that they took drugs to enhance their performance. Those men and women risked everything—their reputation, their health, and the titles they coveted—when they set aside their integrity. And when they were caught, it was a disappointment for millions of sports fans worldwide.

On a local level, maybe you've heard about a city official, PTA president, or manager of a nonprofit organization who took money from a public fund or organization treasury to line his or her own pockets. Or you've seen someone's marriage or business relationship destroyed because one of the partners broke faith. People who make unethical choices may grab hold of success for a moment or even for years, but ultimately they pay a price—the steepest price there is. As I read once, the steepest price a man can pay is his own soul.

IS IT THE RIGHT THING TO DO?

In business, where performance is everything, all too often we evaluate decisions by asking "Is it the most profitable course of action? Is it the easiest?" But how many times do we ask "Is it the right thing to do?" That's exactly what the executives at DaVita asked regarding a clinical decision that would cost the dialysis company a lot of money. Providing dialysis services for almost 95,000 patients in 1,255 outpatient centers around the country, DaVita puts the care of its patients first, seeking to extend life for those suffering from chronic kidney failure. Patients on dialysis go to DaVita centers three times a week to be hooked up to machines that do what their kidneys cannot—eliminate toxins from the body. That means the patients' blood must be taken out of the body, cleaned, and pumped back in. Patients are hooked to the machine through either natural or artificial access. (Natural access involves using the patients' own veins and arteries to create a spot in the body that can withstand the repeated punctures and high volume of blood flow required in dialysis. Artificial access uses synthetic material to bridge between the arteries and veins to create the access.) In the past decade artificial access has become more popular because it is easier for the surgeons to insert. Also, it can be used sooner after surgery (a few weeks afterward instead of a couple of months). However, as time passed, the data revealed that natural access was clinically better for many patients.

Because DaVita believes in taking care of its patients and acting in their best interests, the company took the new data to heart. Each year, DaVita executives and employees vote on the greatest gift it can give its patients. After learning of the superiority of natural access over artificial, the company voted to improve the rate of natural access being used for its patients. To some, that seemed like an impossible goal. Surgeons or specialists are the ones to determine the type of access a patient will get, and that decision is often made even before the kidney fails. By the time a patient arrives at a DaVita center the access is already there, and the company plays no role in the decision.

Yet DaVita was determined to pursue the goal of more natural access for its patients. This decision was not a corporate mandate, but DaVita centers eagerly jumped on the bandwagon because it was the right thing to do. They started education campaigns, explaining to patients the advantages of natural access and hiring consultants to give lectures to physicians on the data. DaVita started to publicize outcomes, influencing surgeons to make the shift. Some centers even told their doctors they wouldn't take a patient with artificial access, unless it was physically inappropriate for that patient to have natural access. Some doctors took offense and referred patients to other centers. The pushback did not deter DaVita. Today, DaVita has more patients with natural access than any other dialysis company in America.

The company faced a similar challenge when Medicare Part D was rolled out. The prescription drug plan was confusing, and many physicians complained that they didn't have time to educate their patients about the new requirements. In a company-wide conference call, DaVita CEO Kent Thiry explained, "We feel a strong sense of accountability for our patients. It's not our responsibility [to educate patients on Medicare Part D] in the strict sense. We didn't ask for this task; we won't get paid for the time we spend doing it. But for so many of our patients, we're the only people who can do it, so we will. It's just the right thing to do." DaVita does the right thing because the company cares for its patients. And the patients reap life-changing benefits.

MAKE THE RIGHT CHOICES

We must always remember that every case of unethical behavior comes down to one person making the wrong choice in any given moment. Ultimately, the only things that truly matter are the choices you have made, are making, and will make. But what are those choices based on? What is your foundation? Are you building the "house" of your life on the shifting sands of the need for success at any price, the love of money, a drive for approval that's so strong you'll do anything for someone's acceptance, a "do it if it feels good today" belief, a fear that if you hold to ethical principles you'll finish last, broke, and alone? Or are you choosing to build the foundation for your life on the bedrock of honesty—on clear, ethical principles? Do you have the courage to go against the common trend at times and do what Coach Carter did—make the right choice no matter what the cost?

I believe that doing the right thing is always the right choice simply because it's the ethical thing to do. Even if it's not easy, even if the ethical choice creates pain in the short term, in the long run doing the right thing will always come out right.

A story in the news told of a potentially devastating school shooting averted by a young man doing the right thing. A fifteen-year-old boy at Green Bay East High School in Wisconsin had heard from some classmates that they were planning to go in and kill several of their teachers and classmates. Now, if you remember high school or have children in high school, you know the strong peer pressure not to rat out your friends to teachers or other school officials. But this young man went against peer pressure and told an assistant principal about his concerns. When the police went to the homes of the two classmates, they found rifles, shotguns, twenty explosive devices, gas masks, and hundreds of rounds of ammunition. They also found suicide notes and mannequin heads that the boys had used for target practice. The two classmates had been bullied at school and were depressed. They were determined to "pull a Columbine."

The young man who spoke up may have experienced pain in the short term from his classmates thinking he was a "goody two-shoes" or a "dork" or any of a hundred unkind words that kids can use on one another. But in the long run he can be confident that he did the right thing and saved many lives, including the lives of the two troubled classmates.

In business, doing what's right even if it causes short-term pain is often equated with a loss of money. At PHH Mortgage Corporation, business decision after business decision is based on the fact that something is the right thing to do, even if it costs more. For example, a loan officer in the field might give a customer certain parameters for a loan transaction and the customer meets those conditions. Later, the company executives realize that more information was needed or that PHH couldn't lend at the rate quoted. They always ask themselves, "What's the right thing to do? What would you do if it was your mother's, brother's, or father's loan?" PHH never goes back on a commitment, even if it means a less favorable loan for the company.

Maybe the appraisal on a property doesn't come in on time, and PHH fails to notify the consumer until 5:30 the day before the loan is supposed to close. Rather than withholding that information from the consumer and the agent and scrambling to fix the problem, PHH admits its mistake and closes the loan on time. It may cost PHH thousands of dollars, but the customer will be able to close on the house.

PHH Mortgage has literally bought customers' houses if the company has been unable to fulfill a commitment based on a poor business decision. Many executives might shudder at the thought of operating the way PHH Mortgage does. How can a company possibly prosper when it gives so much money away? PHH Mortgage builds trust by doing what's right because it's right. The result is much greater success than the company would see if it placed profit from individual transactions over ethical execution.

WHAT IS RIGHT?

General Norman Schwarzkopf was the battlefield commander of the coalition forces during the first Gulf War. He is recognized as an extremely effective leader on the field and an inspiration to his troops. General Schwarzkopf believes that the secret to leadership boils down to two simple rules. The first is this: "When placed in command, take charge." Leaders take responsibility, as we'll discuss later. But what do you do once you take charge? The answer is the second rule: *Do what's right.*

Simple, yes? When it comes to defining right and wrong, you'd think that we would all agree on the "biggies"—that we shouldn't lie, cheat, steal, or kill. However, in today's world many people and authorities tell us that right and wrong are relative terms. They believe that what is right changes according to the circumstances. Depending on the situation, telling the truth may cause more harm than good, they say. If my wife asks, "Do I look fat in this dress?" do I tell her the truth? If my kid steals a stick of gum from his brother, why make a big deal out of it? Depending on whether or not my boss treats me well, I may steal from the company or fudge my time card. After all, what does it matter if I tell my wife a little white lie, or I fudge the number of sales calls I made? If I work unpaid overtime, why shouldn't I call in sick even when I'm not? If my kids are hungry, aren't I justified in stealing from "The Man"? What if my job or my life or the lives of my family are at stake? Isn't the greater good to do something unethical so that my family and I can survive? You probably can think of any number of situations in which someone might justify morally ambiguous actions.

These aren't easy questions, and there are no easy answers. But for far too many of us, "situational ethics" is just a fancy way of saying "slippery slope." One lie almost always leads to another—in fact, one study says that every lie you tell usually requires another *fourteen* lies to cover it up. Certainly there are gray areas in life, but there are a lot fewer than most of us would like to believe. Instead of looking for ethics to fit the situation, we need to assess the situation on the basis of a strong, clear set of ethical guidelines.

Society or a situation might call something right or true when it's not. I believe right is always right. Truth is truth. Two plus two always equals four. There is great freedom when we know what is right. We don't have to agonize over what to do in a given situation. We know what is true, and the truth sets us free.

THREE SOURCES OF AUTHORITY

So, how can we know what's right in any situation? There are three different authorities that speak to us whether we are listening or not. The first is *moral authority*. We're not talking about the cultural mores of society defining right and wrong according to the whim of the moment, but the bedrock values of right and wrong that are shared by all civilized peoples, like the "biggies" we mentioned earlier: thou shalt not kill, thou shalt not steal, thou shalt not bear false witness, and so on. Many of us find our source of moral authority in the tenets of our faith. When we live according to moral authority, we know what's right and wrong, and we understand the moral penalties if we take the wrong action.

We also answer to the *governing authority*. This includes the laws of the society in which we live. In a corporate setting, the company policies are the governing authority. There may be nothing particularly moral about the rules of a governing authority. Speed limits on the roads, for example, or corporate policies regarding how much vacation time you're allowed aren't necessarily governed by a moral code. Yet breaking the laws set by the governing authority or your corporation (as long as those laws do not go against moral authority) can lead you to the "slippery slope" of breaking moral laws as well. The Richmond High basketball players were breaking no moral laws when they violated their agreement with Coach Carter to study hard and stay in school, but Carter knew that young men who broke the laws of his governing authority were all too likely to break other laws as well.

However, just because society tells us something is right doesn't make it right. Nazis in Germany believed it was right to send Jews to concentration camps. Societies at different times in history throughout different parts of the globe have thought slavery was right. We have seen the courage it can take to stand up to governing authority when people believe its actions go against moral authority. Thousands of Europeans saved their Jewish neighbors by hiding them from the Nazis. In the United States, African-American citizens stood up against the injustice of discrimination and segregation during the civil rights marches of the 1960s. Any governing authority has to be judged against the moral authority you recognize, as well as by a third force: your *personal authority,* also known as your conscience.

Your personal authority is based on the ethical standards you set for yourself. You create those ethical standards from four building blocks: (1) your programming, the past experiences that have shaped your life; (2) your thoughts; (3) your values; and (4) your actions. All of these taken together build the moral structure of your conscience, and your conscience shapes your character. When you are connected with your conscience, your character will be firm, and you'll find it easier to execute ethically no matter what.

THE POWER OF PROGRAMMING

Each of us comes into this world innocent and open. We are shaped by the people around us and by the experiences of our lives—our "programming." If you grew up with a dad who loves football, you're likely to love football. If your mom made you lots of Italian food, you'll probably love Italian food. But more important is the ethical and moral programming we get from our parents and our peers. If you see your older brother take a dollar out of your dad's wallet and get away with it, you'll draw lessons from that. If you see your mom telling your dad a white lie about how much she spent for a dress, you'll draw lessons from that, too. What if you told your dad the real cost of the dress and your mom got mad at you? You might learn that telling the truth causes pain. Every experience we have shapes us in some way; our responses are programmed into us.

While I use the term "programming" to describe this, in reality we are much more than computers. When I install a word processing program on my desktop computer and then install the same program on my laptop, the two programs will run exactly the same on both computers—today, tomorrow, forever. In human beings, the same events can produce completely different programming.

I once heard a story of a father who took drugs, stole, and was in and out of jail. He had two sons and was very abusive to his family. One son grew up to repeat the same behavior. The other son became a doctor and raised his family in a loving and nurturing environment. Years later, both sons were interviewed. The first son sat in a prison cell while being asked, "How did you end up like this?" The second son was interviewed in his plush office and was asked the same question. Both of them said the exact same thing: "With a father like mine, what did you expect?"

How is that possible? Weren't both sons programmed in the same way? Perhaps. But somewhere in that second son's life, he chose to change his programming by focusing on other possibilities. Maybe he went to the doctor as a child, took a look around, and saw that it was possible to be something other than a thief. Maybe he had a friend with a loving parent and saw that it was possible for family members to care for one another. Maybe he saw a television show about kids getting college scholarships, so he believed it was possible for him. The point is that we can choose our programming by choosing what we allow to sink into our souls and into our belief systems. More important, we can choose to change our programming at any point in our lives.

One young woman named Heather is a clear demonstration of the power of changing someone's programming. Heather learned before she could walk or talk that taking drugs was normal. Her environment was filled with drugs from the time she was born. Both of Heather's parents were drug users—and both were dead by the time she was fourteen. That's when she moved in with her aunt and uncle, also drug users. Heather naturally started using drugs very early in life. At the ripe old age of sixteen she found herself a high school dropout, living on the streets of Southern California.

Heather lived with her grandmother for a time, all the while stealing the older woman's checks and using her credit cards to the tune of approximately $20,000. When Heather's grandmother finally realized what was happening, she kicked Heather out of the house. So Heather went back on the street. At times she was fortunate enough to stay with friends, but not always. Once, when it was raining, she slept in a trash dumpster to keep from getting wet.

Heather collected money for drugs and the little food she ate by panhandling at the local grocery store. If the nickels, dimes, and dollars didn't add up to enough cash for a line of speed, Heather would steal stereo equipment, tools—whatever she could get her hands on—and then trade the goods for drugs.

Heather's moral compass was completely skewed. She had her own sense of right and wrong, which changed depending on what she wanted to do. She didn't believe doing drugs was wrong. It was certainly okay to do drugs at her aunt and uncle's house because they did drugs too. Neither Heather nor the people she associated with had any regard for the law, which she considered to be a set of recommended guidelines and quite arbitrary. If people hurt Heather, she believed it was okay to hurt them. However, if anyone had helped her or if she felt someone was genuinely good, she wouldn't steal from that person. And Heather felt it was important to keep her word. If she promised you something, she would always keep her promise.

It's easy to look at Heather's story and say, "Of course, she thought it was okay to do drugs. Look at how she was raised. She was programmed to behave in the manner in which she did." Your programming may not have involved drugs and lawlessness. Maybe the unethical behavior modeled for you was of a more subtle nature. Maybe you grew up hearing white lies told for convenience or to cover embarrassment. Or maybe you were one of the fortunate ones whose programming was quite the opposite, and you were taught the value of honesty and integrity. If not, your moral compass can be changed. All it takes is the desire to live and act differently. Often it takes someone who cares about you and who is willing to hold you to a higher ethical standard.

Heather's moral compass was changed because someone cared. A family reached out to her, brought her into their home, and started taking her to church. Heather encountered the teachings of Jesus, and her life was transformed. Heather's new family demonstrated profound caring for this young woman, going so far as to legally adopt her when she was twenty years old. Today, Heather is happily married, has a child, and enjoys a vital life of service, working with at-risk teenagers.

If you were fortunate enough to have had good programming as a child, maybe it's your turn to be a positive influence on the next generation. So many kids today are being programmed by connections they make through technology. Cell phones, iPods, and laptops are connecting kids to a myriad of messages—many of them negative—while at the same time keeping them disconnected from their families. Because moms and dads lead their own busy lives, it's easy to let these technological devices act as babysitters. Maybe we all need to slow down and take a look at how we're being programmed and how our kids are being programmed. We need to be open-minded enough to listen to our kids, to notice and understand their needs so we can meet those needs and help program them with words of affirmation and hope.

Many times, kids who rebel do so because they have been programmed to believe that people don't care about them. Deep down, they want to perform well, but they act out in a desperate attempt for attention. I know a teacher who had a classroom full of smart eleven-year-old kids. One in par-

> **Someone is looking to you for inspiration, for support, for leadership.**

ticular refused to cooperate, intentionally disrupting everything that went on. The boy came from a wealthy family and had every material thing he ever needed or wanted at home. Only when the teacher took the time to sit down with the boy and listen to him did she realize that what he really wanted was attention. He wanted to be part of something and to feel valued.

The teacher knew that the boy liked computers, so she asked him to help teach PowerPoint to the class. The boy's whole life changed when the teacher involved him. He started to believe that he had something of value to contribute. His performance completely changed when he was made to feel special and unique.

Is there a child in your life who needs your guidance and attention? Every child wants to feel special and loved—including the "big kids" we see in the street, in our offices, and in our homes. The greatest gift we can give others, both young and old, is our caring and connection and our gentle guidance. Whether you realize it or not, you are a role model for the people in your life. Your every action is being watched. Someone is looking to you for inspiration, for support, for leadership. What we say to others and how we act will lead the people in our lives to do likewise. Like the Pied Piper of Hamelin, we can take people to the highest tower of ethical action or the deepest forest of casual morality and situational ethics. It's our responsibility to help program others to speak and act in the highest manner.

CHANGE YOUR THOUGHTS; CHANGE YOUR LIFE

As you saw from Heather, you can change your past programming by changing your environment, your peers, your attitudes, and your actions. But most important, you must change your thoughts. Your thoughts form the next component of your conscience, or personal authority.

As children we're not in control of what comes into our environment. We can't control the fact that our parents take drugs, or we're brought up in a poor household, or we don't know our dad, or we move around a lot, and so on. But we can control what we think about those events and what we want those things to mean for our lives when we become adults. We can choose to be like the man who became a doctor, rather than the man who became a drug addict. We can change our thoughts and change our lives.

We can start by seeking out sources of better thoughts for ourselves. Read great books. Study the lives of great men and women who inspire you. Put yourself into positive environments. Someone once told me, "Who you hang around with is who you will become." Take a look at the people in your immediate environment. Do they provide you with the kind of positive thoughts that will take you in the right direction? You might join a church congregation or a fraternal or community organization that will uplift you while you help others. There are hundreds of ways you can create positive thoughts for yourself on a regular basis.

It takes a regimen and a discipline to change our thoughts. We must continually choose what we allow to take root in our minds and belief systems. And we must choose the actions that are in line with those beliefs. People who have been in the military didn't go into the army with the preestablished routine of waking up at 4:00 in the morning, doing pushups, and then running five miles—all before breakfast at 6:00. That behavior started with a regimen that became a discipline. Repeated actions become habits. When you habitually do what's right, you are building success through ethical execution.

WHAT DO YOU VALUE?

Whether you realize it or not, the way you think, the way you speak, and the way you interact with others all stem from what you value. The things you value are the things you care about. And the things you care about shape whether your choices are ethical or otherwise. Values are the third component of your personal authority, or conscience.

What do you value? Do you know? If you were to ask most people the top five values of their lives, you might hear something like this:

1. Faith

2. Family and friends

3. Health

4. Career

5. Recreation

Many of you may share those top five, but they may be in a different order, depending on your life circumstances. If you have no money, work and the accumulation of money will move up the list. If you are battling illness, health becomes a priority. Family might not seem as important to you until you experience the loss of a loved one or a broken relationship.

What you say you value and what your actions demonstrate may be quite different. For some insight into your values, pull out your day planner. How do you spend your time? You can pay lip service to valuing family and faith, but if you spend all your time at work or with friends, and you never set aside time to pray or attend church or read the Bible, then your actions are speaking louder than your declared values.

Now, pull out your checkbook or your credit card statement. Where do you spend your money? If you spend all your time and money around work, then that's your greatest value. If the majority of your time and money goes to recreational activities, then leisure time could be your greatest value.

We dedicate our time, money, and emotional resources to get what we consider valuable. Whatever is at the top of your list had better be something you can trust in without a shadow of a doubt, regardless of what happens to you, because you make decisions based on what you value. If faith is at the top of your list, you will make decisions and consequently perform in a manner that is in line with your faith. If you know that family ranks higher for you than career, then you will not make a career decision or take an action that jeopardizes your family. You're not going to accept a job that requires you to travel five days a week, or move across the country and take your kids away from their grandparents, aunts, uncles, and cousins. You're going to turn down a business engagement, regardless of the money offered, if it means missing Mother's Day. You won't even think twice about it because family is one of your top values.

If, however, your top value is something in which you cannot trust, it will point you in the wrong direction. That's when you will fall into all kinds of questionable behavior in an effort to attain success. If, for example, money is at the top of your list, you will be willing to do anything for it. The same goes for prestige or career. If you fudge contracts to get your sales numbers up, eventually you will be caught. You will more than likely lose your job instead of gaining the recognition and rewards you were seeking. The irony is that unethical performance often will move you further away from the success you so desperately want. On the other hand, if you practice business with ethics and integrity—doing what's right simply because it's right—you will build trust with others, and that in turn will increase your success.

If our programming and thoughts direct our moral compass, our values are the north–south–east–west headings on that compass. We need to make sure that what we value will lead us to the "true north" of ethical execution.

YOUR ACTIONS REFLECT YOUR CONSCIENCE

Our values direct our actions, and the ways we act in the world continually shape our personal authority, or conscience. Ethical actions strengthen our conscience. Unethical actions weaken it. It's really that simple. And our actions are directly shaped by our programming, our thoughts, and our values.

It's easier to act ethically when you know what you value. But what about those you associate with? What do they value? If you connect with people—personally or professionally—whose values are different from yours, it can cause you to veer off course. Many who are serving time now for white-collar crimes are there because they associated with a person or business that breached the law. It may have started quite innocently, with someone taking a job at a company, completely unaware of any illegalities. Then he is asked to participate in small indiscretions. Before he knows it, he is in over his head. Sir Walter Scott had it right when he said, "O what a tangled web we weave, when first we practise to deceive!"—or to act without integrity.

Has your business partner, your boss, a client, a friend, or a family member ever asked you to do something unethical? How did you respond? We've probably all succumbed at one time or another to the temptation to cross the line. Caught up in the emotion of the moment and the desire to please others or achieve a certain goal, we go off in the wrong direction. But with a strong and clear conscience, you won't be blown off course for long. You will turn around and once again head toward the way you know you should go.

Someone once wrote, "Your actions speak so loudly that I cannot hear what you say." Our actions are the clearest indicator of the state of our conscience. We all know people who talk a good game but whose actions don't reflect their words. We also know people who tell us how moral they are, but we know they cheat in their businesses, they cheat on their spouses, and they cheat themselves when they say one thing and do another.

According to *The American Heritage Dictionary,* the word *integrity* means "steadfast adherence to a strict moral or ethical code." But the other meanings of the word include soundness, completeness, and unity. Those who have integrity are unified in that their thoughts, words, and deeds are in line with their values and conscience. They are whole individuals. They are people you can trust. I hope you are one of those people. Let your actions reflect your values and your conscience, and you'll experience the wholeness that integrity brings.

CHARACTER IS A CHOICE

How you act in the world, how your conscience plays out in the bigger arena, determines your character. For you to execute ethically, the most important thing you can equip yourself with is good character. It is the underpinning for every connection; it should be the underpinning for your life. My grandmother would always say, "A good name is better than great riches." Yet we are under so much pressure to perform today—in business and in our personal lives—that it's easy to succumb to shades of gray when we try to achieve something of great importance. But if you succumb, you risk forfeiting your good name and losing the character that should be the very foundation of your life.

Character is a choice you make each and every day. The following diagram shows what I mean.

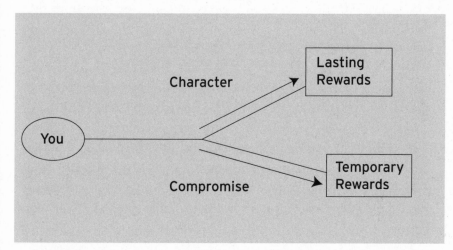

Let's say it's 5:30 in the evening on Wednesday, and you're driving back to the office after meeting with a client. You're looking forward to heading home after a long, hard day. Then you notice that the message light on your cell phone is blinking. You dial into voice mail and hear a message from your boss, telling you there's a big error in some of the figures that you and your co-worker, Joe, used in the quarterly sales report. He wants you and Joe to stay late and fix the mistake. You know that Joe is back in the office, probably hard at work on the report. But your spouse is waiting for you at home, and you promised you'd be home for dinner for a change. You could easily pretend you didn't get the message and go straight home, leaving Joe to fix the report by himself. After all, he's single and not likely to have a lot planned for a Wednesday night, right? When you see him tomorrow, you can tell a little white lie about not getting the message, and no one will be the wiser.

You're at a fork in the road where you can make the ethical decision or the expedient one. You can take the high road of character or the low road of compromise. Compromise means you save the message and head home. You get the temporary reward of an evening with your spouse, but you've left a colleague in the lurch. It may feel good, but it's not the best choice in the long term.

On the other hand, you can choose character over compromise, call Joe, and tell him you'll be there in fifteen minutes, then call your spouse and explain why you'll be late. There may be short-term pain associated with the choice of character, but there also are long-term rewards. You supported a colleague. You fixed something that you had taken responsibility for producing. You kept your commitment to your boss and your co-worker. You didn't have to lie. You made the ethical choice when it was easier to compromise. And ultimately that will always make you feel better.

We're faced with these small moments of choice constantly, but even if they seem small, the consistent choices we make will determine how ethical we are. When the cashier rings up the wrong amount for your purchase and it's lower than the actual cost, what do you do? When you unload your groceries into your car and there's no drop-off station for the shopping cart nearby, do you leave the cart in the middle of the parking lot or do you walk it back up to the store? When you're at a restaurant, do you pocket some extra sweeteners or a few mints? Have you ever taken a towel from a hotel room? What about supplies from work? The company has so many pens that they'll never miss a few. Or you worked overtime the other night and didn't document it, and you think you deserve that stapler as compensation. It won't make any difference, you tell yourself. But did you know that employee theft (yes, taking that stapler is theft) accounts for billions of dollars in losses for companies in the United States every year? What do you suppose is the markup in retail just to cover employee theft? What is the cumulative impact of all those people who took "just one" pad of sticky notes from the office?

Maybe the collective losses played a role in downsizing. Maybe the impact was one person's job.

You can justify such actions all day long. Kids have a long list of reasons why they choose to cheat in school. "Everyone else does it." "The teacher grades on a curve, and since other students are cheating, I have to cheat in order to make it fair." "I need to cheat so I'll have the grades to get into college." "I don't have time to study." "It doesn't matter if I learn what they're teaching, because I'll never need to use it in life." "Besides, it's not hurting anybody else." What those students don't realize is that their actions *are* hurting others as well as themselves. The truth is that everybody else doesn't cheat. If that teacher grades on a curve, more than likely the honest ones will suffer. Grades earned through cheating are meaningless if nothing is learned. Students who take that path will have a rude awakening in college and in life when they realize they did need to know that math after all. Studying takes discipline. Learning the art of discipline will serve these students in countless areas throughout their lives. The bottom line is this: if you cheat, there are consequences. Every action has a reaction.

What if a camera were on you twenty-four hours a day, broadcasting to the world everything you do? How you treat your family, your friends, your fellow worker, your customers, the waitress, the driver in the car in front of you, the tollbooth worker, the custodian? Would you be proud of your actions? What would they say to the world about your character?

MAKING DIFFICULT CHOICES

Our character is shaped most strongly in the moments when we are called to make difficult choices. When someone poisoned several boxes of Tylenol in the 1970s, Johnson & Johnson pulled Tylenol off the shelves of every store in America. The company ran TV commercials urging people to stop taking its own product. This ethical action cost Johnson & Johnson millions of dollars, but it kept the trust of its customers strong.

Johnson & Johnson revamped the packaging for its over-the-counter painkillers to make them tamper-proof. When Johnson & Johnson ran ads a few months later to let the public know what it had done and to assure its customers of the safety of Tylenol, millions began taking it again. The customers believed in the tagline of the commercial for the product: "Trust Tylenol." Consumer safety and maintaining its reputation of trustworthiness is more important at Johnson & Johnson than the almighty dollar. Do you think this has negatively affected the overall success of Johnson & Johnson? Hardly. For generations, Johnson & Johnson has been a household name, and it continues make *Fortune*'s list of the top five most respected companies.

Sometimes doing the right thing requires personal sacrifice. But the reward is always worth the cost. Undoubtedly there will be times when you do the right thing and it causes you or other people pain. For example, owning up to a mistake is never easy. Being the only one in your crowd to say no to another drink is not pleasant. You can be called a prig or a stuffed shirt or holier than thou if you're not willing to accept your company's fudging its numbers or painting a rosier picture than what you know is true. But if you feel pain because you've done the right thing, think of this: when you're on your deathbed, how will you view your choice to act ethically? Most of us would prefer to endure short-term pain if we know the long-term consequences will make the sacrifice worth it.

> **Sometimes doing the right thing requires personal sacrifice. But the reward is always worth the cost.**

Gandhi said, "A man is the sum of his actions, of what he has done, of what he can do. Nothing else." The good news is that you can choose your actions. Every day you wake up to a clean slate, a brand new day in which to start all over. You don't even have to wait till morning: you can do it right now. Every moment is an opportunity to choose the right path for the situation.

TAKE IT PERSONALLY

Acting ethically doesn't always mean sacrificing a relationship. Often acting ethically strengthens our relationships with others, especially when we treat people the right way. Anthem Blue Cross and Blue Shield has created a culture in which it has become second nature for call center employees to do what's right because it's right. People at Anthem understand that health care and health insurance are very personal matters. When Anthem customers call, it is because they are sick. They need care and attention. Call center employees can easily put themselves in the shoes of the person on the other end of the line, so they respond to their customers' needs with care and empathy.

At Anthem Blue Cross and Blue Shield, those who take care and empathy to another level are referred to as Service Heroes. These heroes take a customer's plight to heart. They take it personally, then they do what's right because it's right. For example, if a customer has just been diagnosed with an illness and the pharmacy doesn't have her insurance information, the call center employee will stay until 7:00 at night if that's what it takes to resolve the situation and get the customer's prescription filled.

Nicole Russell had the opportunity to do what was right when she got a call from a customer with multiple sclerosis (MS), a chronic disease that requires medication on an ongoing basis. The customer's insurance benefits, however, had an upper limit on how much could be paid for her medications. She reached the end of her prescription coverage in May. With seven months left in the year and no way to pay for the high-priced medications, the customer called Anthem in distress.

Nicole could have said, "That's what our benefits offer, and that's all we can give you." But she didn't. Nicole empathized with the devastation this customer felt from living with a disease that caused unimaginable hardships each and every day. The medication just to make her life bearable was so expensive that she had maxed out her insurance benefit in only five months. So Nicole took it upon herself to contact the major pharmaceutical companies that manufacture the medications the customer needed. For several days, Nicole spent hours of her own time, off the clock, to research the various assistance programs offered by pharmaceutical companies in which the medications could be provided at major discounts, if not free of charge. Nicole was able to connect the Anthem customer with a vendor to get her the medications she needed at no cost once the drug cap was met each year.

IF YOU DO GOOD,
FEEL IT!

Stories like Nicole's are commonplace at Anthem Blue Cross and Blue Shield. Nicole didn't have to sacrifice her time and efforts for a woman she didn't even know, but she did it because it was the right thing to do. And it paid off—for the woman with MS and for Nicole.

What is the benefit to Nicole? It goes back to personal authority. When you do what is right, you know it, even if no one else does. Nicole's conscience told her it wasn't right to hang up the phone without trying to help that customer, especially when Nicole knew there were supplemental programs out there that could possibly provide a solution to the woman's dilemma. The Anthem customer was elated when Nicole's actions helped her obtain critical medications. But doing what was right also made Nicole feel good.

Don't we all feel good about ourselves when we do what is right because it's right? Doing what's right creates a sense of self-worth and builds self-esteem. When we do right for others, we are doing right by ourselves.

REWARDS OF
INTEGRITY

When you come to a fork in the road, the choice to make is yours. Will you choose character or compromise? To stay true to your convictions, you first must have some. That's why it's important to look inward and define what it is you value. If your values aren't where you want them to be, it's never too late to readjust your priorities and, as General Schwarzkopf says, start doing what's right.

Ethical or unethical choices are not confined to just one aspect of our lives. If we lie at work, eventually we will lie at home. If we cheat in sports, we will more than likely pocket the extra change the cashier mistakenly hands us. If our moral compass points away from integrity, we will be led that way to some degree in just about every circumstance. When we follow that direction, we can be certain of one thing: ultimately, we will not win.

Conversely, a moral compass that is pointed toward ethics will not only reap material rewards but also reap the reputation that comes with good character. It will reap a good name that lives on beyond you. It will reap blessings in the lives of others. And it will reap a spirit of optimism, inspiring others to follow your example in doing what is right.

EXECUTE ETHICALLY
ACTION STEPS

1. What examples have you seen in your life or in the media of people and companies that have sacrificed integrity for the sake of performance? What were the results of their actions? What would you have done if you had been in their shoes?

2. Make a list of what you consider moral truths. What are the immutable principles that you believe should underlie an ethical life? What are you willing to use as your personal authority, or conscience?

3. Do you have programming in your past that needs to be changed? Were you brought up to think it's not that bad to take a few things from work, or to lie about an extra-long lunch hour or a date with someone your parents didn't approve of? If you have thoughts and programming that lead you away from character, you can change them with affirmations, reading ethical texts, attending church, and so on. Fill yourself with new programming and thoughts, and you'll find it easier to make ethical choices.

4. Take a few moments to make a list of your top five values. Now, look at the ways you spend your time and money. Do you need to revise your list to reflect your genuine values?

5. Do the people around you reflect the kinds of values and actions you want to emulate? If not, you may need to find other people to be around.

6. Think of a situation in your life in which you have had to choose between the high road of character and the low road of compromise. Which one did you choose? How did

you feel? What would have happened if you had made the other choice?

7. Fill in the blank: **ICARE to take action now by executing ethically and doing what's right in the following ways:**

_____

CONNECT Step 6:
Challenge Your Challenges

Do what you can, with what you have, where you are.
—*Theodore Roosevelt*

Does the word *challenge* give you a queasy feeling in the pit of your stomach? Does the adrenalin start to flow? Do combined emotions of fear and uncertainty start to pulse through your veins? If so, consider yourself completely normal. For a lot of us, challenges create fear—and with good reason. Challenges are hard! They rock our world. They disrupt our plans. They wreak havoc. No matter how hard you try, you simply can't escape them. Challenges come in all shapes and sizes. Your age, your nationality, where you live, whether you're married or single, whether you're the most admired or the least admired—none of these matter: challenges are part of life.

Maybe your life has been one challenge after another for as long as you can remember. Or you could be one of the fortunate few for whom life seems to roll along with hardly a bump in the road. But then, out of nowhere, disaster hits and your world crumbles. You lose your job and don't know how you are going to pay your rent or mortgage. You may have lost a loved one, faced illness, gone through divorce, cared for elderly parents, or dealt

> **"Just because challenges come, they don't have to overcome."**
>
> **—Dr. Creflo A. Dollar**

with rebellious children. Perhaps you feel overwhelmed and pulled in so many directions that your relationships, health, and work are suffering.

Maybe you face increasing pressure to perform on the job. Company budgets are tightening in an effort to hit revenue goals, and you're being asked to do more with less. If you are a leader or manager in that type of environment, perhaps you have trouble pulling your team together to accomplish a seemingly impossible project. The challenges your team faces are affecting morale and work quality in the most negative ways.

How do we respond to the challenges in our lives? Many times our first instinct is to run away. But when I'm faced with challenges, I remember what my pastor, Dr. Dollar, says: "Just because challenges come, they don't have to overcome." No one succeeds in the face of difficulties by lying down and giving up. We've got to respond to challenges with our strongest efforts. I believe the word "challenge" should empower us and make us more eager to enter the fight. We must rise to the occasion, bring our best to the table, and challenge the challenges we face. The sixth CONNECT principle is to *challenge your challenges*.

We all have challenges to overcome in our lives, but it's how we choose to meet them that will make the biggest difference. When a challenge comes your way (and it will), instead of running *from* the challenge, run *to* it. Meet that challenge head on. Residing within you are the power and purpose to help you fight any challenge and beat it. When you step up, challenge your challenges, and strive to overcome them, you connect with yourself and others at the deepest level.

There was a compelling commercial on television not too long ago. Cycling great Lance Armstrong, seven-time winner of the

Tour de France, looks straight at the camera and says something like, "Remember me, cancer? You gave me less than a fifty percent chance to live. You made me suffer; my mom, too. But you made me what I am today." Lance Armstrong was a top cyclist when he was diagnosed with testicular cancer that had spread to his abdomen, lungs, and brain. He chose to undergo aggressive chemotherapy, losing all his strength and much of his lung capacity in the process. For the next two years he struggled to regain his cycling prowess. But he battled back and in 1999 won his first Tour de France, followed by six more victories. Lance Armstrong confronted his challenges head on. He gave cancer no chance because he was so strong and took complete responsibility for doing everything possible to get healthy again. Armstrong has won many awards and races, but I'll bet he would tell you his greatest victory was challenging the challenge of cancer.

BE RESPONSIBLE *AND* ACCOUNTABLE

The BE-Attitude for this step is to *be responsible*. How many challenges in our lives would be overcome if only we would take responsibility? That character trait seems to be harder and harder to find. People today tend to point fingers and shift blame, or look to someone else to take care of their problems. These are the slackers who don't want to shoulder responsibility for their lives and the challenges they face. When we look around, we see far too many slackers and not enough owners— individuals and organizations that deal with challenges as they arrive. *The only way you are going to challenge the challenges in your life is to be responsible for them.*

Earlier in this book, we talked about CONNECT Step 1, Commit to win, and its BE-Attitude, BE accountable. The first step of connecting is always to make a decision, commit to acting upon that decision, and then be accountable for the results you produce. But being responsible goes beyond being accountable. Accountability means that you are willing to be measured by your results. Responsibility means that you take ownership not just of the individual results but also of the outcome for which those results are achieved. In a battle, for example, soldiers are accountable for doing the fighting, but their commanders and generals are responsible for the outcome of the battle itself. In your life, you must be accountable for your results and responsible for how those results affect your life and the lives of others. Responsibility links you and your results to bigger outcomes.

Let's look at a business example. Say you're part of a sales team that covers a certain territory. You're accountable for the number of calls you make, the clients you see, and the sales you close. But you're also responsible to your team for holding a high standard in your sales, for doing your best, for supporting the other team members, and for producing results that will increase the numbers for the entire team. You're responsible for supporting the team's outcomes as well as for making your individual sales goals.

I read once that *responsibility* is composed of two separate words, *response* and *ability*. We all have the ability to choose how we will respond in any given situation. When we're responsible, we are calling on more of our abilities so we can respond rather than react. Responding usually requires that we connect to something beyond our immediate impulse. We tune in to our higher values, for instance, or perhaps to our purpose in the situation, or perhaps to the needs of others in addition to our own. Responding allows us to connect purpose, people, and performance in one seamless flow.

Being responsible—that is, able and ready to respond—can be measured in three ways. First, you must *show up ready to do your best*. Second, you must *respond rather than react*. Third, you must *make the right choice*. When all three factors are present, you will respond in ways that will allow you to challenge the challenges that life places in your path.

SHOW UP READY TO DO YOUR BEST

Being responsible requires that you not only show up but also come prepared to give your all. In sports it's called putting on your game face. Every athlete knows that in order to conquer the competition, he or she must be prepared to give everything to the effort of that day's game, track meet, or match. You must show up ready to be your best. Any lesser effort is not being responsible to your team, your supporters, or yourself.

The same thing holds true in business. Have you ever known someone who was just going through the motions on the job? Have you had a team member who didn't pull his or her weight in working on a project? You know how that kind of attitude can drag down both the spirit and the results of the entire team. Challenging challenges requires that we are responsible for bringing our "A" game to work. When all team players show up ready to do their best, then everyone's job is more enjoyable, even if the team faces hard times.

Showing up ready to do your best comes in many forms. It always starts with an internal check. Only you know what your best is, and only you know when you're bringing your "A" game to work or when you're slacking off. After you've done your internal check, however, you're going to be measured against external standards. You can feel that you're doing your best on the job, but if you're not getting your work done on time or you're skipping steps or not communicating with your team members, then according the demands of the job you're performing below par. You've got to know the standards of excellent performance in your area so you can measure yourself against them and meet them to the absolute best of your ability, no matter what.

I was in a cab recently, and the cab driver asked me what I did. I told him I was a motivational speaker and corporate trainer, helping people and companies develop a winning attitude.

"Let me ask you a question," the driver said. "What do you do in the mornings when you get up and you just haven't got it? Do you ever not feel like getting out there and motivating people?"

"Sure," I told him. "But I'm also responsible to my clients and my audiences. They're relying on me to be at my best and to deliver what I've promised, and I will never let them down if I can help it."

"So, how do you turn it on?" he asked me.

"Let me tell you about the last presentation I gave," I replied. "I was just in Kansas City, and I'd been traveling and speaking for about two weeks straight. I had to do a speech for about eight hundred people at 9:00 AM. When I got up in the morning, I prayed for an hour and then got dressed, but I realized I wasn't ready to go yet. I didn't have the energy I needed to move people to achieve a winning attitude.

"So I made the choice to drive myself to that state. I visualized where I needed to be and the energy and excitement of my message. I used my voice and body in such a way that I felt that energy. Then I put on my suit coat and left my room. One of the housecleaners was standing in the hall next to her cleaning cart. Now, the acid test of my state is always the moment when I see somebody. So I smiled my biggest smile, and with all the enthusiasm in the world I said to her, 'Good morning!' She looked surprised but said 'Good morning' back. I walked down the hall to the elevator, and when the doors opened, I said to the four or five people inside, 'Good morning, everybody! Thanks for picking me up!' They answered, 'Good morning!' and smiled at me.

"By this time I was almost at the state I needed. I walked down to the ballroom, and about twenty people were waiting outside. I said to them, 'Here he is!' with a big smile on my face. I was ready to go onstage and do what I had to do. I'm in the people business, and I'm responsible for inspiring and motivating folks to be the best they can be, so I have to be the best I can be when I'm with them. That's how I take care of business."

When I get out of bed on a morning when I'm scheduled to speak, it doesn't matter whether I feel like bringing my "A" game or not. I know the internal standards I will demand of myself, and I also know the external standards my audience will demand of me. I do whatever I need to do to match my internal and external standards before I step out of my room. I put on my game face and go out every day ready to give my best. I consider that not only my responsibility but also an honor and a privilege. You, too, should consider it an honor and a privilege when you are called upon to bring your "A" game to the playing field of life. I hope you feel the call inside yourself every day, because when you consider yourself responsible for showing up at your best, then you're living a life that will be powered by people, purpose, and high performance.

DON'T REACT: RESPOND

The second measure of responsibility is to *respond rather than react*. You have the ability to respond to a challenge instead of reacting to it. But responding takes a willingness to pause and think. Reactions usually bypass our brains. They're snap judgments, punches thrown in a bar, cruel words that leave our mouths without any warning. And while reactions are important when we're in immediate physical danger, most of the time reacting instead of responding can cause all kinds of trouble.

Let me give you an example. Imagine that a colleague comes by your office and tells you he overheard John talking to a friend at a competing company about the new "hush-hush" product your team is developing. You're furious—you've been working on this project for two years, and any leaks may mean that your competition will bring out a version of the product first. You storm over to John's cubicle and say sternly, "Come with me." You walk him into your office and ask him point-blank if he's been talking to the competition. John denies it, of course, but you tell him that someone overheard him. Now John gets defensive and angry because people have been eavesdropping on his "private" conversations. You argue for several minutes before John declares, "I can't work under these conditions!" and leaves.

Later that afternoon your colleague comes to you, chagrined. "I thought John was talking to his friend Mary over at our competition," he tells you. "Well, I just found out he was talking to Mary in our branch office in Texas. He was filling her in on the project so she could give him some input on the rollout." You're embarrassed and ashamed. You go to apologize to John, but the damage is done. Two weeks later you find that John has accepted a position with your competition.

What if you had responded to the report about John instead of reacting from your emotions? If you had thought a few moments, you might have asked yourself questions like this: "What else could this mean? Do I have the full story? Does this report jibe with what I know about John, who's a loyal and dedicated member of our team?" You could have questioned your colleague further to make sure his facts were accurate. You could have had a quiet word with John just to clear up a "misunderstanding" instead of accusing him of leaking company secrets. If you had responded instead of reacting, you might have kept a valuable employee.

This may be an extreme example, but how often have you reacted emotionally when told something about someone instead of using your brain to respond? When you take a moment to let your brain weigh in before taking action, you usually find that far more choices are available to you that will allow you to challenge whatever challenge presents itself. "Our behavior is a function of our decisions, not our conditions," Stephen Covey writes. When you address challenges in a constructive manner instead of reacting to negative conditions around you, you can overcome most of the challenges you face.

BE A VICTOR, NOT A VICTIM

When we are faced with significant challenges, it's all too easy to feel that we're victims of circumstance. But that is one of the biggest traps we can fall into. Victims are overcome by their challenges, not the other way around. When Lance Armstrong received his cancer diagnosis, he quickly declared that he wasn't a cancer victim—he was going to be a cancer survivor. He was determined to overcome cancer instead of letting cancer overcome him. To challenge your challenges you must change from victim to victor. You must declare victory over your circumstances no matter how terrible they may be.

One woman exemplified that mind-set in an amazing way. You may or may not recognize the name Trisha Meili. At twenty-eight, Trisha was the picture of success. With two graduate degrees from Yale, she was working as an investment banker and had her eye on a vice presidency at Salomon Brothers. Then, in a matter of moments, her life was changed forever.

For fourteen years Trisha was known only as the Central Park Jogger. In April 1989, she was brutally attacked in New York's Central Park. She was left for dead after being raped and severely beaten. To the surprise of doctors and all who saw her, Trisha didn't die. However, when she awoke from a twelve-day coma she had lost her ability to walk, talk, identify simple objects, and tell time. Severe brain damage had left her in a condition that would have defeated most people.

Her body was shattered, but amazingly, her dreams were not. Trisha says that from the beginning she felt like a survivor, not a victim. Rather than plummeting into depression, she threw herself into a stringent rehabilitation program. She challenged herself to respond rather than react to every obstacle

> **You must declare victory over your circumstances no matter how terrible they may be.**

> **Responding instead of reacting transforms us from victims to victors.**

she faced. Before her rehabilitation was even complete, Trisha went back to work at Salomon Brothers. She got that vice presidency she longed for. And those first small steps she took in rehab grew into bigger ones. In 1995, the woman no one thought would live, let alone walk again, ran the New York City Marathon. Trisha's experience inspired her to leave the corporate world and write a book about the hope and perseverance that pulled her through. Today, Trisha Meili is a sought-after speaker, inspiring hope in others.

When faced with a horrific situation like Trisha's, most of us would feel completely justified if we reacted with depression and anger. Her circumstances were unfair, unjust, and unbearable. But we learn from people like Trisha that there is power in responding rather than reacting. Responding means that we take time to think, to assess, and to ask questions that will allow us to look for the best in any situation. Responding allows us to find resources we never knew we had—resources we will never have access to when we're stuck reacting to events. When challenges hit, don't react and play the victim. "I lost my job. I don't know what to do." Well, how did you get your first job? You had a resume and went on some interviews. Instead of reacting by sitting around and feeling sorry for yourself, get another resume and start making calls. Respond by putting your heart and soul into the "job" of finding the work and workplace you've always dreamed of. Responding instead of reacting transforms us from victims to victors.

MAKE THE RIGHT CHOICE

In the previous chapter we talked about doing what's right because it's right. But doing what's right isn't always easy, especially when we're faced in the moment with a choice between a painful right and an easy wrong. I believe that the very definition of responding instead of reacting means that we can stop ourselves from choosing the easy way instead of the right way. Responding means that we can let our conscience weigh in on the choices we make. We can be responsible and consider the long-term consequences of our choices instead of simply going for the short-term gain. We can let our values and purpose guide our actions. When we are responsible for making the right choice, we will challenge our challenges in ways that make us feel good while we do good.

Not too long ago my doctor called me to cancel an appointment I had made for a surgical procedure the following day. We'd had the appointment for months, and it was the only day I was in town and my calendar was free, so I had to ask her why she was canceling. "I'm sorry, Keith, but my twelve-year-old son broke his arm, and he has to stay home from school tomorrow," she told me. "I feel I should stay home and take care of him when he's in pain. I'm truly sorry for the inconvenience. When can we reschedule your appointment?" I know my doctor is a dedicated healer and hated having to cancel appointments, and she knew how hard it had been for me to schedule this surgery. But on this occasion her responsibilities as a mother were more important than her professional role. I appreciated her choice because she felt she was doing the right thing. I also felt she was acting responsibly toward me because she let me know why she was canceling our appointment and gave me the opportunity to reschedule at my convenience, not hers.

When we're responsible, we show up ready to be our best, we think before we act, and we endeavor to make the right choice that will create the greatest good for ourselves and others. If there ever was a recipe for challenging our challenges, I'd say that was it.

THE SIX THINGS YOU MUST DO
TO CHALLENGE YOUR CHALLENGES

I'm not saying that it's easy to challenge the challenges that life throws your way. But I do believe that our challenges are given to us so that we will learn and grow. If we don't challenge ourselves physically with regular, vigorous exercise, our bodies get flabby and out of shape. People who face few challenges in their lives can end up flabby in other ways—mentally, emotionally, and spiritually. We were put on this earth to serve great purposes and to accomplish great things. We can't do either unless we are strong and tested.

The U.S. Navy SEALs are some of the most highly trained and elite fighters on the face of the earth. Their training regimen is so stringent that up to ninety percent of recruits leave the program. The first five weeks of SEAL training are filled with intense physical and mental conditioning. Recruits are subjected to an endless series of push-ups, sit-ups, pull-ups, ocean swims, and timed four-mile runs in boots and long trousers. They're put into groups of six or eight in crews that routinely handle boats of up to 150 pounds. The third week of their training is infamously known as Hell Week—seven days designed to stretch men to their breaking points and beyond. Recruits are subjected to endless physical stress—constant runs, swims, boat drills, and calisthenics—all on a total of four hours of sleep for the entire week. The men are constantly wet, cold, tired, covered in sand, shot at with blanks, screamed at, and verbally abused by their instructors. Any recruit can drop out of the program at any point. Many do—but many also elect to come back and try again. Recruits have gone through training as many as three times before passing. That's how strong their drive is to become a SEAL.

Navy SEALs know that they can withstand the greatest challenges and emerge victorious because they have been tested in the harshest of conditions. It's unlikely that you will have to face that kind of physical extreme—but you can learn from the SEALS the six keys for challenging the challenges that arise in your own life.

1. You must face reality

Many young men aspire to become Navy SEALs, but when faced with the reality of Hell Week, many drop out. Now, think about the recruits who drop out and then reenroll in the training! They already have faced the reality of what they must undergo, and they choose to go through it anyway. When facing a challenge, you must be very clear about the problems and difficulties it brings.

It can be difficult to acknowledge a challenge and the circumstances that brought it on, because it means facing reality—and facing reality is rarely pleasant. Some of us in the workplace are slow to acknowledge the competition or a change in culture or a change in our market. In our personal lives, we don't always want to face the reality of broken relationships, financial hardships, or life-threatening illnesses. It's much easier to look at the bright side and to be optimistic about a challenge. Don't get me wrong: I'm all for optimism and a winning attitude. But a positive attitude is not the same thing as delusion, and it doesn't mean ignoring cold hard facts in favor of pipe dreams. You've got to see things as they really are. Regardless of the magnitude of a challenge, you must acknowledge it. Only then can you develop an attitude that will help you win in spite of—or perhaps because of—the challenges you face.

Start by assessing your challenge. What is it really? What are its circumstances? What obstacles does it represent? Get very clear about the components of the challenge you're facing. Make a list of the facts as you know them, and determine exactly where the biggest obstacles lie.

Say you've just been handed a project at work that's due in a week. Two of your key team members have just taken off for a week's vacation and are not available. Budget cuts mean you can't bring in a lot of outside subcontractors to help. You're going to have to pull this off with short staff and limited resources.

Now, you must be honest about yourself. What physical, mental, or emotional obstacles are you experiencing as you face this challenge? Be gut honest. There's a difference between honest and gut honest. When you are gut honest, you can't fool yourself. And with knowledge comes power—*if* you have the wisdom to use what you know. If you need help, admit it. Call upon others to help you. Connect with people who will support you emotionally and who can support you with skills you may be lacking to accomplish your goal. Let others help you. It's not a sign of weakness but a sign of strength.

Let's go back to the work project. When you're honest, you may realize that while you could get the project done with your current resources, it would require you to work twenty hours a day for the next week. The amount of physical, mental, and emotional strain probably would affect the quality of your work. You also notice that you're very resentful at having this project dumped in your lap by your boss, and this makes you less inclined to work hours and hours of overtime to get it done.

Based on your honest assessment of yourself and the challenge, you may decide to do several things. First, you ask some of your colleagues if they could spend a couple of hours helping you to gather the data you need for the project. You enlist the support of some of the administrative staff and company interns. If they will put in some time to help out, you'll mentor them in doing the job and help them acquire skills that they can use in their future careers. You ask your spouse to support you as you work the longer hours, promising you'll make up for it after the project is completed. You go to your boss and state clearly your plan to get the project accomplished. You also let him know that in the future you will ask that he give you more notice and/or take into consideration vacation schedules and staffing needs when assigning important projects like this one. Finally, you make a commitment to yourself to spend a half hour every lunchtime at the gym so you can keep your physical health on track.

Facing reality is responding rather than reacting. It's allowing our brains to override our emotions so we can see the challenge for what it is—not bigger or smaller, but of its real size. When we do that, we can tailor our efforts to match the requirements of the obstacles we face.

2. You must have the right mind-set/attitude

Navy SEALs train their bodies, of course, but more important, they train their minds. To challenge your challenges, you must cultivate the right mind-set. And that starts with belief. You must believe in your purpose, in yourself, in your abilities, and in your potential for overcoming obstacles. Belief and mind-set helped Trisha Meili accomplish amazing feats. Belief and mind-set inspire athletes to perform beyond their abilities. If they believe it, they can achieve it.

The truth is that whether you think you can do something or think you can't, you are right either way. Too often, thinking "I can't" becomes part of our DNA. It shows up in our vocabulary, the way we dress, our demeanor, how we walk, how we talk to ourselves. Psychologists say that upwards of eighty percent of most people's internal dialogue is self-defeating. You see it in sports teams from Little League to the pros, or in sales teams, or in entire organizations for that matter. Restructuring a losing DNA is a difficult task—but not an impossible one.

Ron Martinez, a Senior Vice President at Bank of America, did just that. He came to Bank of America from outside the banking industry and took charge of a low-performing region that included East Los Angeles and South Central Los Angeles, where the Rodney King riots had taken place. Eighty percent of Los Angeles area gangs were in this area. No one believed that this region, with its low income and predominantly Hispanic population, could become one of the top-performing Bank of America markets in the country. No one, that is, except Ron.

Refusing to be dragged down by the skepticism surrounding him, Ron encouraged his team members to believe in themselves and their abilities to overcome the challenges in their region. He coached them to be world champions. He connected with his team members, and he endeavored to notice and understand their needs as well as the needs of his customers. He then mapped out a plan and took action to provide the tools needed to turn the vision into reality.

Ron not only believed in his team but also believed in the potential of his customers. He established a Bank of America community resource center in East Los Angeles—the first such Bank of America center in the area. Some might have thought it was a waste of time to invest that kind of capital in the Hispanic neighborhood. But Ron believed. He did his homework and found that his customers' kids were learning about computers in their schools. He thought, why couldn't these kids teach their parents? So the community resource center was filled with PCs. Online banking shot through the roof as kids stood with their parents, showing them how to use the computers. And because many Mexican immigrants who settle in East Los Angeles are looking for work opportunities, the resource center also offered seminars to teach them how to start a small business and obtain financing (through Bank of America, of course).

In only a year and a half, Ron's region went from eighty-eight to number two in the country. Ron's success started with his own belief. Then he could coach others to believe as well. With belief behind them, Ron's team members overcame enormous obstacles and achieved outstanding results.

Ron Martinez was surrounded by naysayers; yet he developed the beliefs and drive to take his region to the top. If you're not able to call on others, or on those on your team, you have to look inside. You have a very powerful team of your own, made up of Me, Myself, and I. You are not alone. You have the spirit within you. Look inside yourself. Stir up momentum. Like belief, momentum and motivation have to take root on the inside. So look inside and find it.

Look to your own past. Go back as far as your memory can take you. Remember the times you challenged a challenge, no matter how small. Think about when you learned to tie your shoes, when you took your first test in school, competed in the spelling bee, had your first date, went to college, got your first job. Notice the recurring appearance of the word *first* in that list? The first time is usually the most challenging. What did you do when you overcame those first challenges? You did it before. You can do it again. Hold on to your successes, and each time you face a new challenge, your fear will diminish and confidence will grow. You can do it if you believe there is a champion inside of you.

Belief starts with your internal dialogue. Make sure you're saying the right things to yourself. Believe that you are destined for greatness. Tell yourself that over and over again, because it's true. Tell yourself you can do something, and you will change your attitude. What used to be viewed as a challenge, you will see as an opportunity, a stepping-stone to reach your destination. Change your attitude and you will change your feelings. Change your feelings and you will change your action.

We all have control over our internal programming. It starts with what we say to ourselves. What if you woke up every day and counted your blessings? Many people like to keep gratitude journals to remind them of all their blessings. Start in the morning by focusing on all the little things you're thankful for, and by midday you'll be in a state of joy. You must be careful not to let outside influences rob you of that joy. Monitor your programming by monitoring what you let into your mind—from what you see on television to what you read to the people you choose to surround yourself with.

We all have problems. Some are bigger and tougher than others. But every problem has within it the seeds of opportunity. The real challenge is simply getting from where you are today to where you want to be. When you look at a problem as an opportunity, your mind-set begins to change, and that spark of hope becomes a fire in your spirit. You will start to believe, and your DNA will begin to transform. You will have the confidence to overcome anything. It's called the Big Mo in sports—the momentum that carries teams to new heights of success. Ron and his team experienced it. You can, too—with the right mind-set, the right belief, and the right internal dialogue.

3. You must know your internal motives/drivers

It takes courage and motivation to drive through obstacles and to be responsible for your actions. But where does motivation come from? It comes from your internal motives/drivers. The word *motive* is defined as that which incites a person to take action. The driving power that enables you to push through even the most difficult of challenges is different for everyone. When you tap into your personal motives, you drive yourself into action.

Our internal motives help trigger the emotions that drive us to be responsible. However, as my good friend and mental toughness coach Steve Siebold reminds us, corporate executives all too often neglect to consider the role emotion plays in business. He writes:

To connect and overcome a challenge, whether in sports, business or in your personal life, you must start by being mentally tough. That means you must look at the dual roles of logic and emotion. When we're talking about business strategy and business acumen, it's important to come from a place of left-brain logic. But when it comes to motivation—the willingness to push forward and persevere—we must talk about emotion. People should be guided strategically through logic, but we are all motivated through emotion. Making that distinction is critical.

The greatest internal driver is love, which motivates us to care. If you love your kids—if you care about them—you're going to work the number of jobs you need to in order to provide for them, even if it requires sacrifice. If you care about your team, you'll work long hours and pick up the slack for co-workers who might be having problems. If you care about your purpose and vision, as we discussed in an earlier chapter, you'll put in the effort needed to attain both. When you define your motives—the emotions that drive you—and find out what motives and emotions drive others, you will stir up the momentum that motivates people to accomplish the impossible.

4. You must have a plan and act upon it. You must know How, What, and WIN

To be truly responsible, you can't simply sit around and wait for things to happen to you. You must decide how you want to respond and what you are capable of doing, and then take the actions required for creating success. You must have a plan and act upon it. And your plan must include *How, What,* and *WIN.*

How

Your plan starts by asking *How*. How are you going to face this challenge? Will you constantly remind yourself that what's inside of you is greater and stronger than what's outside of you? How are you going to respond to the situation? How much do you care? Is the end result worth fighting for? All too often we can spend a lot of time, effort, and psychological energy on responding to something we really don't care all that much about. You must weigh the costs and decide whether whatever lies on the other side of a challenge is worth pursuing. Or perhaps there's another way to obtain the same result.

Seventeen-year-old Adrienne was always very clear about how she wanted her particular dream to come true. As far back as she could remember, she'd wanted to go to college on a basketball scholarship. However, she was only five feet two inches tall, and in the world of collegiate women's basketball, she'd be competing against women eight to twelve inches taller.

In high school, Adrienne was a great basketball player and a key player in her school's championship team. As the end of the fall basketball season approached, scholarship offers for her teammates were rolling in. But Adrienne's phone didn't ring. By late winter, not one school had shown interest in her. She was dejected. Her first thought was that it was a sign. Perhaps she shouldn't continue to fight so hard for this goal. But then she stopped and asked herself *how*. How important was the scholarship to her? How would it fit in with the purpose and vision for her life?

Adrienne looked around at the inner-city high school she attended, and she knew she wanted more. Playing college basketball was worth fighting for. Whatever it took, Adrienne resolved to find a way to live her dream. So she took responsibility and formulated a plan. She and her mother purchased a book that listed all the college athletic departments in the country. Adrienne made a list of her own, outlining what she was looking for in a college. She wanted a small school in either a town or a rural community. She also wanted a school that offered a good business program.

Adrienne sent out letter after letter to the schools that met her criteria, asking for questionnaires and offering to send basketball tapes highlighting her athletic ability. No response. Though disappointed, she did not give up. She knew her reasons were too important to allow her to give up. "Who cares that I'm only five-two," she thought. Adrienne had proved her ability to compete on the court. She now proved her determination as she continued to mail out letters, approaching fifty to seventy different colleges.

In spite of her admirable efforts, the end of the season arrived and there was still no offer. Emotion began to well up inside Adrienne as she played what she thought would be the last few games of her basketball career. She played as she always had—with all her heart. Finally, beyond all hope, the call came. A small Division 1 college in Maryland offered Adrienne a scholarship, which she happily accepted. Adrienne fulfilled her dream of playing college basketball and paving the way to achieve much larger goals throughout her life. Adrienne went on to earn a master's degree in sports administration.

Adrienne started by asking how, which helped her to challenge herself in the face of great obstacles. When facing your own obstacles, keep asking questions to discover how you are pursuing your goals. What do you want to do? For whom do you want to do it? And for what purpose? How will feel once you achieve your goal? If your answers are strong enough to motivate you to pay the price, then get to work. You have the fuel you need to generate the momentum that will keep you moving forward.

What

Action is all about *What* you will do. This is where the planning part of the equation comes in. Map out your goals. Create a plan. Identify what help or resources you need. Remember, you are not merely a human being but a human becoming. What is it you want to become? What regimen do you need to follow to make that happen? It could be mental, physical, or spiritual—or all three.

Your plan might involve daily disciplines. Athletes who compete in a triathlon don't wake up one morning and say, "I'm going to go for a 2.8-mile swim. Then I think I'll ride my bike 100 miles and finish with a 26.2-mile run." They start with a plan that helps them take the first step. That first step might be walking a couple of blocks before they jog a half mile. Maybe it's swimming one lap before they can do several laps. Or riding their bike a couple of blocks before they can conquer a couple of miles. Remember, action starts with the first step and with the discipline to continue acting on a daily basis.

WIN

Accomplishing any task requires that you stay focused on *WIN*: What's Important Now. Start by identifying the steps you need to take, and then break your task down into smaller pieces. When life serves you an enormous challenge, you don't need to solve the whole thing all at once. But you do need to handle a little bit at a time if you are ever going to take care of the challenge. Don't let distractions disconnect you from the task at hand. Focus on that one action you are taking rather than the whole endeavor, and you won't be overwhelmed. Remind yourself of your purpose in attacking this goal. Go back and read what you wrote when you answered why the goal was worth pursuing.

Then repeat it to yourself over and over again. Envision what your life will be like on the other side.

Action also requires that you learn from your progress. Challenges by their very nature are tough. The road to overcoming them is rarely easy. But you must use your experiences to learn more about yourself and the challenge so that each step becomes easier. Stephen Covey once wrote, "Our most difficult experiences become the crucibles that forge our character and develop the internal powers, the freedom to handle difficult circumstances in the future and to inspire others to do so as well." When the challenge that seeks to destroy you instead makes you stronger, that's what we call transforming turning points into learning points.

It comes down to being responsible for that challenge. Challenges attempt to turn you off course, which will disconnect you from your goal and from others. You must respond to all challenges and take the appropriate steps to learn from them and grow stronger.

5. You must have hope

In the midst of what may seem to be life's most impossible challenges, there is always reason for hope. There's an old saying: "Hope for the best; prepare for the worst." When you have hope, you hold the picture of the best outcome in your mind while you take the actions needed to conquer your challenge. Hope is the emotion that will propel you forward in the most difficult circumstances.

For American Express, a company that had created a niche in travel and entertainment spending, the terrorist attacks of September 11, 2001, dealt an especially devastating blow. With travel curtailed and businesses cutting back, many at American Express took on an attitude of doom and gloom. Ken Chenault, however, saw things differently. Having just taken over as CEO only nine months before the attacks, Chenault faced what most saw as an impossible challenge with optimism about the opportunities at hand. Determined to infuse that attitude throughout the organization, he met with employees and continually drove home a message of hope and possibilities. Chenault's confidence was contagious. Less than a year later, American Express had bounced back, and it began a solid growth streak that continued for several years. Chenault responded to incredibly challenging circumstances with mental toughness. He looked for opportunity and he found it. He expected the positive rather than the negative, and he inspired the entire company with his hope and enthusiasm.

While it's important to be realistic about the challenges we face, it's equally important to keep a positive attitude about our chances of overcoming them. Only with hope can we access the mental and emotional resources that lie within us. Only with hope will we be able to look for the best while we prepare to handle the worst. Hope will light our path to victory over our challenges.

6. You must persist and persevere

Of course, hope isn't enough to get us through challenges. We must act upon our hopes. More important, we must persist and persevere in the face of ongoing obstacles. Persist means that we refuse to give up. Persevere means that we are steadfast in purpose. With persistence and perseverance, we can overcome almost anything.

Ed Doherty is the king of persistence and perseverance. You may remember Ed from earlier chapters. As President of Doherty Enterprises, Inc., he owns more than sixty franchise restaurants, including Applebee's Neighborhood Bar & Grill, Chevys Fresh

Mex, and Panera Bread Bakery-Cafés. But Ed's first job out of college was as a sales representative for Mobil Oil Corporation. If Ed had illusions of grandeur upon entering the workforce with such a respected company, he was quickly brought down to earth. His territory placed him right in the middle of Brooklyn's crime-ridden neighborhood of Bedford-Stuyvesant.

Ed's job was to call on gas station dealers in Bedford-Stuyvesant to sell oil, gasoline, tires, batteries, accessories, and the like. That year race riots had broken out in cities around the country, and every day Ed was walking right into one of New York's most notorious areas for violence. To say he wasn't warmly greeted is an understatement. The sales rep working the territory before Ed had lasted all of two weeks. It had been months since the dealers had seen a Mobil representative. Day after day, Ed was thrown out of all forty stations in his territory.

Of course, Ed was frustrated and a little concerned about his physical safety. But he didn't let his frustrations or fear get the best of him. He went back. Each and every week, Ed put on a suit and tie, took a deep breath, put on a smile, and drove into Bedford-Stuyvesant. Over and over, he called on the stations in the broken-down neighborhood, asking if there was anything he could do to help. Sometimes it meant going down to the deli and getting a cup of coffee, or down to the local auto parts store to pick up some spark plugs. "I can sell you some spark plugs," Ed would offer enthusiastically. "For years, Mobil Oil did nothing to help us out, so I'm not buying anything from them," a dealer would snap. "Just go get me the spark plugs!"

A month passed. Then six weeks. Then eight. Suddenly, one of the dealers had a change of heart. "You're always here," he said to Ed. "You're a pain in the neck, but I'll buy some oil from you." Slowly but surely, all the dealers followed suit and started buying products from him. Ed was ecstatic. He might not have been selling much dollar-wise, but when he compared his numbers with previous sales in that territory, his percentages were

> **Choose your strategy to suit your challenge.**

off the charts. Mobil management sat up and took notice. Ed became a hero within his district and division.

Why didn't Ed just quit, as those before him had done? An only child who had been raised by a single mom, Ed had watched his mother struggle as she worked diligently to support the two of them. Throughout her life, she owned her own businesses and worked around the clock. She overcame tremendous challenges and inspired Ed to do likewise. Failure simply wasn't an option.

Failure will do one of two things: it will paralyze or it will mobilize. In Ed's case, it mobilized. He became mentally tough, took responsibility, and formulated a plan to overcome his obstacles. He had a job to do, and he was driven to do that job to the best of his ability.

If you've ever seen sculptors at work, you know that they use many different means to shape the block of stone or marble. Sometimes they take a hammer and chisel and hit one massive blow, and a large chunk of stone falls away. Other times they tap delicately, slowly, creating a small crack that becomes larger and larger until eventually they remove the extraneous stone. As you work on your own challenges, you can conquer them either by breaking through or by whittling them down a stroke at a time. Choose your strategy to suit your challenge, but always remember that persistence and perseverance will be rewarded.

TEAMWORK WILL TRIUMPH OVER CHALLENGES

One of the best ways to challenge the challenges you face in life is to build and support a team with the same dreams and goals. Great leaders and businesses know that teamwork will help everyone triumph over the most difficult challenges. Great companies also understand that a team is created not simply with common professional goals but also by caring about the personal challenges each team member faces. For instance, the culture at Monster, the leading global online careers site, is uniquely supportive in helping people overcome challenges. Monster does more than accumulate resumes and find jobs. The company has a noble purpose: "Bringing people together to advance their lives." This means working together to challenge both life and work challenges. Brian Graham, formerly Senior Vice President of Enterprise for Monster, explains it this way:

> We understand that a key part of business success is to help employees with their personal challenges. Monster is an organization that allows people to express themselves. It's okay to share that you have a challenge and need help. Cancer, a death in the family—it could happen to any of us. Even the happier scenario of being a first time mom or dad has its challenges. It's okay to take time off if you have a personal need or crisis. We know that when you come back, you'll be rejuvenated. We treat others the way we want to be treated. It's a powerful message and creates a sense of fairness and team. As a result, our retention rate is through the roof. People stay because they know we genuinely care.

In sports and in business, momentum is created when a team is all on the same page. It is the responsibility of the leader to instill that sense of team when attacking challenges. Martha Corder, a Regional Vice President at one of the top five pharmaceutical companies in the world, took over a team that had nowhere to go but up. Her region was ranked twenty-fourth out of twenty-four in the country. But Martha believed in her team and their ability to turn things around. She talked to her team members and discovered what they believed were causing the problems in the region. Martha asked for their input, letting her team members know that their opinions held merit. This created in the team a sense of ownership—not only of the challenge but also of the company itself. Martha motivated her sales team by connecting them to a greater purpose. She reminded team members that their work contributes to making the world a better place. No other industry changes humanity in the same way theirs does. She infused in her team members the belief that what they do has far-reaching implications.

Martha continually built up the team with positive reinforcement, acknowledging the challenges at hand as well as the successes in tackling those challenges. No matter how small the win, she let her team members know that their hard work was appreciated. She treated her team members like winners, and they started acting like winners. The team started getting things done and left the bottom regional ranking to climb several steps up the ladder of success.

Martha said of working with a team:

> When analyzing a problem, if people feel you are trying to place blame, they will shut down. But if they feel like it's a collaboration of great minds, tackling an issue so everyone can be more successful, you're going to get buy-in. They need to feel like we can't do it without them. And we can't. What they are contributing to the process is of great value. I know my team is talented. I know they are extremely well trained. I know they are strategic and I know we can get things done.

We are all inspired when we see or hear about others who have gained victory over a challenge. If we open our eyes and look around, we can see people pulling themselves up by the bootstraps with the determination to succeed. We see in these individuals a vision and a desire to overcome obstacles. And, as in the case of Ed Doherty, we observe a daily discipline that helps a person reach predetermined goals. As we watch others who turn challenges into opportunities, their mind-set becomes contagious. We think, "If someone else can overcome that big a challenge, so can I."

When you are going through a challenge, look around and determine who can give you insight or inspiration. There is always someone within your reach to give you the tools you need, to motivate you and stir up hope. Perhaps you're facing a personal challenge and don't have the luxury of co-workers to share the responsibility of finding a solution. You might have to call a friend, or find a mentor with knowledge that you need. Maybe you've read about someone who has overcome a challenge similar to yours. Grab your inspiration there. Or think back to your past. Did you know someone who experienced the same problem? What was it that carried that person through? If you don't remember, pick up the phone and find out. Build an A-team of individuals you trust with similar values and a shared vision. With their support, you will be able to challenge any challenge that comes your way.

Challenges today are far greater than they have ever been, and they are not going away. But if you adopt the six ways of challenging your challenges—if you face reality, adopt the right mind-set/attitude, know what motivates and drives you, develop a plan and act upon it (knowing How, What, and WIN), have hope, and persist and persevere—when the next challenge comes knocking at your door, you will have the confidence and the skill to turn it into an opportunity of amazing proportions.

CHALLENGE YOUR CHALLENGES ACTION STEPS

1. Recognize that challenges are a part of life. When faced with a challenge, run toward your challenges, not from them.

2. The only way you are going to challenge the challenges in your life is to be responsible. Own your responsibility for dealing with your challenges. Don't let yourself be caught in the blame game. How does it feel to say to yourself, "I own these challenges; I take responsibility for how I deal with them"?

3. You must master the three measures of responsibility. First, you must show up ready to do your best. How do you define your best when it comes to the challenges you're currently facing?

4. Second, you must understand the difference between responding and reacting. Have there been times when you reacted and regretted it afterward? How could you have responded in those situations?

5. Have you ever allowed yourself to feel like a victim of your circumstances? How else could you have responded, and how much better would you have felt?

6. Third, you must make the right choice. What's an example of a time when you didn't make the right choice in a challenging situation? What's an example of a time when you did choose the right path?

7. Take a look at a challenge or an obstacle you're currently facing. It can be at work or in your personal life. Use the six ways to challenge your challenges to help you handle this issue.

8. Start by facing reality. Describe the challenge in very clear and dispassionate terms. Don't minimize it, but don't blow it out of proportion either. What are the physical, mental, or emotional affects of this challenge? Who else does the challenge involve?

9. Once you're clear on the challenge, what mind-set/attitude do you need to develop to handle it? What beliefs do you need? What experiences from your past might help you with this situation? What internal programming or dialogue do you need to use to keep your mind-set positive and proactive? Create a winning mind-set/attitude for yourself, and you'll be amazed at how much easier it is to develop momentum.

10. You now know your mind-set/attitude; now you need to add the emotions that will keep you motivated. What are your motives/drivers? What feelings will juice you and help you charge into each new day with determination and perhaps even excitement?

11. Now, what's your plan? Evaluate every challenge: *How* will you face it? *What* steps must you take to defeat it? *What's Important Now?*

12. How can you create hope for yourself and anyone else involved in dealing with this challenge? Hope is belief in a brighter future and in a successful outcome to your efforts. Hope doesn't mean that you stop acting; hope helps you continue to take action in the face of all odds. With hope on your side, anything is possible!

13. With hope must come persistence and perseverance. Hope propels you forward, but perseverance keeps you fighting when the going is tough. What disciplines must you develop to persist over the long run?

14. Challenges are best fought by teams. Draw upon the teams you already have, or create a new one to help you challenge your challenges. Who do you need to help you fight the good fight? Call upon help when needed.

15. Fill in the blank: **ICARE to take action now by being responsible and doing** _____

_____

to challenge the challenges in my life.

CONNECT Step 7:
Transcend Beyond Your Best

If you do what you've always done,
you'll get what you've always gotten.
—Anonymous

In CONNECT step 1 you heard a little bit about my friend Art Berg. I met Art for the first time in Orlando, Florida, at a conference for professional speakers. A few years later we were both delivering over 170 talks a year. We always wanted to connect but never had the chance or time to get together. However, one day I picked up the phone to hear, "Keith? This is Art Berg. I'd love to spend some time with you. Not too many people can relate to how hard it is to be on the road and maintain a level of excellence as a speaker. I want to learn from you. When can we meet up?" A couple of weeks later I was in Dallas, Texas, and heard a knock at my door. There was Art in his wheelchair. He was speaking in Texas and had rented a car and driven an hour and a half just to meet me! Within five minutes we really connected. Art was one of the best speakers on the planet. While he had said he wanted to learn from me, every time I talked with him I came away with incredible lessons, both practical and inspirational.

Art told a story about the time he attended his young daughter's school play. At the end of the play all the kids asked their parents to give them the thumbs-up sign—but with his paralyzed hands, Art couldn't manage it. So his daughter ran out into the audience and held her dad's thumb up for him. That became one of his signature stories. One year I spoke at a company where Art had spoken the previous year. When Art told the story of his little girl, it inspired the company so much that they instituted a "Thumbs Up" award given each year to the employee who helps others the most.

Art passed away at the age of only thirty-nine, but his spirit and inspiration live on in everyone who knew him, read his books, or heard him speak. Art was the best example I know of CONNECT and the BE-Attitudes. He committed to achieving whatever he set his mind to, and he was accountable to himself and others for producing results. He opened to opportunities and embraced change even when it was as difficult as accepting that he would never walk again.

He noticed what was needed and necessary in every situation. Once I read a story about a question-and-answer session after one of Art's talks. A young woman in a wheelchair had the microphone, but she was having trouble getting her question out. The usher took the microphone and was moving on to someone else when Art motioned him to give the mike back to the young woman. "You take all the time you need," he told her with a smile.

Art navigated his entire life by his purpose, and his strength came from being vision centered. He built a successful career by executing ethically and doing what's right because it's right. He challenged incredible challenges and was responsible for achieving the impossible. And most important, Art transcended: he went beyond his best to make a difference for the hundreds of thousands of people who heard him speak. Art Berg truly went beyond the circumstances of his life to make an impact on the world. He demonstrated the power of the seventh step of CON-NECT: *transcend beyond your best.*

THE DRIVE TO TRANSCEND

Transcend is not a word commonly used in life or in business, but I choose it specifically because of what it means. To transcend means to rise above, to go beyond, to exceed, to surpass, to excel. When we transcend, we go beyond challenging our challenges; instead, we rise above them and achieve a level of success that we never before thought possible.

This is not to say that we ignore our challenges or circumstances. Art Berg could never ignore the fact that he was paralyzed. Someone who's been out of work can't ignore the fact that he or she needs a job. In business, if you ignore difficult circumstances you'll probably be out of business before too long. But when you transcend, you learn in the deepest part of your being that you are much greater than anything that can happen to you. You learn there is a source of strength inside you that can pull you through no matter what your outside circumstances may be.

Deep down in the spirit of every living, breathing human being is the drive to transcend. Transcending gives us hope and brings hope to others. It brings significance to life. Transcending is about triumph and victory. It's about discovering more in ourselves and creating more in our businesses. In his best-selling book *Good to Great,* Jim Collins describes how some companies go beyond what most people think of as "best" to reach levels that only the most successful enterprises attain. When you go beyond your best and CONNECT to the steps in this book, you will live a life of meaning while you experience greater success. When we transcend our challenges and go beyond the expectations of ourselves and others, we automatically create greater success through people, purpose, and performance.

Throughout this book we've told you stories of people who have transcended beyond their best and made a difference. Maybe as you've read these stories you've started to implement some of their practices. I hope you've discovered the benefits these principles can bring to your life. But when you take the final step of recognizing that you can rise above any circumstance, that you have the strength and will and heart inside you to overcome any challenge, then you will connect at the deepest level with the spirit that lies within us all—the spirit that transcends any problem. When we recognize the true source of our strength, we discover that we can do anything.

Transcending also can mean sticking by your principles even when they might cause you pain, in the belief that your actions will produce the highest outcome. I'd like to tell you about a businessman who did exactly that. S. Truett Cathy is the founder and CEO of Chick-fil-A, the second largest quick-service chicken restaurant chain in the United States. Mr. Cathy has been in the restaurant business since 1946, when he and his brother opened a tiny café next to a Ford Motors plant in Hapeville, Georgia. The café had ten stools at a counter and four tables, and it was open twenty-four hours a day, six days a week, to accommodate plant workers. But Mr. Cathy, a devout Christian, always closed his restaurant on Sundays to honor the Sabbath and allow time for church activities.

In 1967 Mr. Cathy opened the first Chick-fil-A fast-food restaurant in a shopping mall in the Atlanta, Georgia, area. At the time, it was easier for Mr. Cathy to keep to his rule of closing his restaurants on Sundays, since most malls were not open for business on Sundays either. But as the chain expanded into other cities and states, some businessmen questioned the wisdom of losing Sunday sales. In 1982 a mall developer offered to make a donation of $5,000 for each Chick-fil-A restaurant that stayed open on Sundays, the donations to go to a church of Mr. Cathy's choice. But Mr. Cathy stuck by his principles, and to this day all Chick-fil-A restaurants are closed on Sundays.

In 2005, Chick-fil-A had more than 1,280 restaurants in thirty-seven states and Washington, D.C. The chain sold more than 156 million of its signature white meat chicken sandwiches, and it reported sales of more than $2 *billion* in one year. Still a family-owned business, Chick-fil-A has increased its sales for thirty-nine consecutive years. But Chick-fil-A has set itself apart from other fast-food restaurants not just by its results. The chain produces more sales in six days than its competition does in seven.

S. Truett Cathy held firm to his principles even though industry leaders said that closing on Sundays would result in lost business. Mr. Cathy rose above the expected requirements of business to make a profit at all costs by doing what he believed was right according to his faith.

TRANSCEND AND MAKE A DIFFERENCE

Transcend may be a word that few people can relate to; yet they are going beyond their best on a daily basis. Parents who take time off from work to care for a sick child are transcending. Team leaders in business who allow those parents to take time off, and the team members who take up the slack for their missing colleagues, are transcending. Every time we ask forgiveness, or forgive a wrong done to us, we are transcending. Every time we succeed despite the odds, we are transcending.

The BE-Attitude of this step is to *be the difference.* If you've ever done something for other people to help them raise themselves up, you know how great it can feel. It connects you to yourself and your real purpose on earth like nothing else.

In this chapter you'll hear about many people and businesses that have gone the extra mile and acted according to the greatest commandment of all, that we love our neighbors as ourselves. I hope you will take their examples as guides for transcending beyond your best and being the difference in any and every circumstance.

TRANSCEND BY LEARNING FROM ADVERSITY

We all experience adversity in some shape or form. The ones who transcend are those who say, "I am going to make something of myself in spite of my circumstances." That was Nido Qubein's belief. The young man was only six years old when he lost his father, but he was fortunate to have a mother who inspired him to make the most of his resources. Nido came to America from Lebanon as a seventeen-year-old who didn't speak English or know a soul in this country. With fifty dollars in his pocket, he enrolled in college. Determined to succeed, Nido worked ten hours a day while going to school. At the same time, he learned English by putting ten words on a three-by-five card each day and studying them, giving himself a day off on Sundays. At the end of the year, he had 3,120 words in his vocabulary—62.5 percent of the 5,000-word vocabulary of the average American.

Adversity is what you make of it, and Nido transcended it. Nido Qubein is president of High Point University in North Carolina. He has written fifteen books, which have been translated into twenty languages. He has been inducted into the Speakers Hall of Fame by the National Speakers Association, and he has received the highest awards given to professional speakers by that organization. Nido is also the chairman of several companies, including Great Harvest Bread Co., McNeill Lehman (a national public relations firm), and Business Life, Inc.

Recently Nido Qubein was honored with the Horatio Alger Award for Distinguished Americans. The award is given to people who have come from humble beginnings, overcome adversity, and gone on to accomplish great things. Nido joins fewer than three hundred living Horatio Alger Association members in the world.

Nido has been the difference in his own life by transcending adversity and attaining abundance. He has taken obstacles and suffering and turned them into something positive. He has learned from difficulties and become better because of them. Nido's life tells us that anything is possible when we make the most of our resources.

TRANSCEND BY CARING

If you think your obstacles are too hard to transcend, you may want to talk to Dick Hoyt, who has pushed his wheelchair-bound son, Rick, over the finish line of every Boston Marathon since 1981. Father and son also have competed in several triathlons, including the most notorious of all, the Ironman in Hawaii. What makes this story even more inspiring is that Rick has absolutely no use of his arms and legs and cannot speak. He communicates using a computer.

Dick, a retired lieutenant colonel with the Air National Guard, is now in his sixties; yet he continues to undergo vigorous physical training. He needs it if he's going to compete in triathlons where he must (1) tow his son on a raft while swimming 2.4 miles in the ocean, (2) ride 112 miles on a bicycle with a chair attached to the front where Rick sits, and (3) run 26.2 miles while pushing his son's wheelchair.

Ever since Rick was born a spastic quadriplegic with cerebral palsy and unable to speak, Dick has worked with great determination to give his son every opportunity. Dick and his wife refused to take the advice of doctors to put Rick away in an institution. Instead, they raised him as normally as possible, even getting their son admitted to public school. When Rick was fifteen, Dick pushed the young man in his wheelchair in a five-kilometer

> **The energy of your caring and commitment can carry you through adversity.**

race. Rick's words to his father, communicated via computer, set the course for the next three decades. He typed, "Dad, I felt like I wasn't handicapped."

Why does Dick do it? The love and caring he feels for his son. At the core of everything we've talked about is caring. That's what makes organizations successful. It's what makes all the people we've profiled in this book successful. When you care, you are empowered to tap into your potential and transcend daunting obstacles. In the case of Dick and Rick Hoyt, it has brought victory. Not the victory of crossing the finish line first—instead, Dick and Rick Hoyt have overcome mediocrity, fear, and the limitations that well-meaning people have tried to place on them both. Their victory lies in going beyond their best and accomplishing the "impossible."

You, too, can have that kind of victory. You can rise above a family disagreement, or someone else's negative attitude, or someone's mistreatment of you. You can overcome the fact that you're overweight, or you have a drug problem, or you had a traumatic childhood, or your boss hates you, or your competitor is acting unethically. You also can overcome more insidious enemies such as laziness or a tendency to settle for the status quo. How do you do this? With the power of caring. The energy of your caring and commitment can carry you through adversity, helping you rise above the circumstances of your past and present. When you tap into the power of caring you will discover how much smaller even the biggest obstacles can seem. Caring will help you go beyond your best and be the difference.

TRANSCEND BY PURSUING EXCELLENCE

I once heard about a hair stylist in Columbus, Ohio. When he announced he was moving to New York City, his clientele were absolutely distraught. They couldn't imagine going to another hair stylist. Completely taken aback by their reaction, he told his customers they would be in good hands with the other stylists in the spa where he worked. But to a person his clients said, "It won't be the same without you." What made the difference? This stylist had a degree in chemistry, and he would tell clients how the different chemicals used in perms, coloring, and so on were affecting their bodies. He also had friends who were doctors, so if a client had questions about a medical condition related to their hair, skin, or scalp, he would ask his doctor friends and report back on their comments. This gentleman went above and beyond for his clients. He is a great example of transcending by pursuing excellence in everything he did.

Maybe you've been fortunate enough to be on the receiving end of care that pursues excellence. Have you ever had a doctor who actually called you at home to see how you were doing after an office visit? How about a customer service representative who spent thirty minutes on the phone with you in a real attempt to resolve an issue? If you have, how did you feel afterward? Pursuing excellence usually means going beyond what you have thought of as your best and also beyond what other people consider the best. Pursuing excellence creates a "wow" experience for all concerned. Your customers say, "Wow! He or she really went above and beyond." Your co-workers say, "Wow! I never thought we could be successful with that project or sales goal." And you say to yourself, "Wow! I never knew I had it in me!" When you go beyond your best in the pursuit of excellence, you'll find that success is usually the natural result.

TRANSCEND BY GIVING
FROM THE HEART

One of the best ways to transcend is to give from the heart. We all respond to the call to give because it allows us to tap into the highest part of ourselves. Giving feels good! That's why people reach out to help in the face of disaster. People feel that they just want to do something—anything. And so they do. Donations pour into the Red Cross. Individuals sacrifice time, money, and efforts to load up buses and airplanes with food and medical supplies. During times of war, a steady stream of care packages makes its way to our soldiers who voluntarily put themselves in harm's way. There is something in all of us that wants to be the difference. It's that part of us that wants to transcend beyond our best.

When we give from the heart, we come to understand the true meaning of the words "It is better to give than to receive." A technology brokerage in Connecticut was deeply affected by the loss of life on 9/11. Employees at the company had lost several friends, colleagues, and family members in the attacks. The brokerage wanted to do something to help the families affected by the tragedy, so the company decided to donate all the proceeds from one day of trading—normally around $500,000—to the families of those killed in the attacks. The most the company had ever netted in one day was $1 million. But when the brokerage told its clients what it intended to do, the response was overwhelming. That day, the brokerage raised over *$6 million.*

Giving from the heart usually calls us to go above and beyond. In business, whenever you link the power of caring with the pursuit of excellence, inevitably you will produce exceptional results.

TRANSCEND BY SMALL ACTS OF KINDNESS

As wonderful as these stories are about others going above and beyond, it's easy to be intimidated by those who seem to epitomize the concept of transcending. "I'm just one person," you say. "And I'm no Mother Teresa!" You may think you can't make a difference, but think again. Even the smallest gift can have great value when it's given from the heart. It can be as simple as extending a helping hand, or saying hello to brighten someone's day, or even helping your neighbor get through a crisis. It could be giving someone a ride, a smile, or a word of encouragement.

The people at HCR Manor Care understand how simple it is to be the difference. HCR Manor Care cares for the elderly and ailing in more than five hundred skilled nursing centers, assisted living facilities, outpatient rehabilitation clinics, hospices, and home health care offices across the United States. Horror stories about the state of many skilled nursing centers are all too common, but HCR is dedicated to providing the best caring in addition to the best care. That's why you hear stories like that of the HCR Manor Care nursing assistant who stayed at work after her shift was over to spend the night with a dying patient. Or workers who tuck patients in, kiss their foreheads, and say "Sweet dreams" every night. Or nursing assistants who work in one of the lowest-paid professions in the country and still take money out of their own pockets to buy gifts for their patients.

Such acts of kindness are commonplace at HCR Manor Care because employees are taught that it's okay to care. The tendency for many in the health care industry is to put distance between themselves and their patients. If they don't, they hurt too much. HCR Manor Care is different. Employees believe it's a privilege to get close to their patients, to connect with them, and to care. Every patient who enters an HCR Manor Care center is matched with a "Guardian Angel," a staff member who takes time getting to know that patient and any family members. The Guardian Angel personally responds to that patient's needs with acts of kindness, making the patient feel especially cared for. Sometimes those acts of kindness involve gifts; other times it's the gift of a smile and a listening ear.

Sometimes responding to a patient's needs means granting heartfelt wishes. The Heart's Desire Program at HCR Manor Care takes caring for patients to yet another level. When Guardian Angels or other HCR Manor Care employees learn of something a patient has always dreamed of doing—or would like to do again—they make it happen. The stories of dreams fulfilled range from attending a NASCAR race to going on a special fishing trip to celebrating Christmas in September so the patient can be with family members. It's no wonder that HCR Manor Care facilities are some of the most sought after in the country. When people and organizations transcend, they can bring joy to even the most difficult of situations.

About twenty years ago, HCR Manor Care decided to create a customer service/guest relations program. The result was Circle of Care, which has become the cornerstone of the company culture. Circle of Care is about caring for people—patients and employees alike. Training programs focus on teaching the staff to go "above and beyond" in listening, communicating, and respecting the patients, their family members, and HCR Manor Care employees.

After going through the Circle of Care training, an HCR administrator we'll call Mary began to notice that a longtime employee, "Kristy," was missing work and coming in late. One day Mary looked down the hallway and saw Kristy, who looked worn out physically and emotionally. Mary walked over to Kristy and instinctively gave her a hug. Every day after that, whenever she saw Kristy, Mary gave her a hug. Slowly, Kristy began to open up to Mary, coming into her office to chat.

In Mary's office, Kristy finally poured out her heart. She said, "This year is the tenth anniversary of my husband's death. My daughter recently left home to go to college, and my son moved out two years earlier. I've been all alone, and I thought I had nothing to live for. The only thing that has kept me going was caring for my patients. But after a while, even that was not enough. Two months ago, I came to work with the intention of gathering up my belongings, going home, and taking my life. That was the day you hugged me for the first time. That hug began to pull me out of my depression and enable me to go on."

It's amazing what a simple hug can do. Of course, it was more than that: it was the care behind the hug. Mary took the time to notice. She created a safe atmosphere for sharing. And she took a genuine interest in what Kristy had to say. It started with caring, and it ended with saving a life.

To be the difference, you don't need to lead armies or create a movement that will change the world. You can transcend and be the difference with almost any small action. Can you bring a coffee back for a busy co-worker? Give a compliment to an unsung hero or heroine on your team? Stay fifteen minutes late to make sure a client receives the order on time? Your smallest actions can be the biggest difference in creating a connected and powerful relationship between you and others, especially when those actions come with no expectation of reward.

An old joke asks, "What's the best way to eat an elephant?" The answer is, "One bite at a time." To transcend and be the difference you don't need to lead a movement or add a million dollars to your company's bottom line. Instead, you take one small action that makes a difference in someone's life or makes one customer happier. When you practice taking these kinds of small steps, they add up to a big difference. More important, they start to become a way of life, and before you know it, transcending has become your natural state.

TRANSCEND BY GIVING ANONYMOUSLY

Have you ever done something without asking for recognition? Committed an act of kindness and remained anonymous? One anonymous giver walked along the streets of Los Angeles, looking for expired parking meters. No, she wasn't a meter maid. She was putting quarters in the meters of total strangers, then rushing away so no one would catch her committing this act of kindness. We can't know the specific circumstances that prompted this woman to save drivers from parking tickets, but you can bet on one thing: she received the satisfaction of knowing she was making a difference.

Perhaps that is what spurred someone to give anonymously to Nido Qubein, whom you met earlier in this chapter. After Nido had learned English while working his way through two years of junior college, the time came for him to transfer to High Point University in North Carolina. Then he got some surprising news. The college president called Nido to his office and said that while Nido thought he'd made enough money to cover all of his school expenses, it wasn't enough. However, the president added, a doctor who lived nearby had volunteered to pick up the tab for the difference.

Completely overwhelmed by the gesture, Nido asked who the donor was so he could express his immense gratitude. But the college president said that the doctor wanted to remain anonymous. Nido went back to his dormitory, knelt by the side of his bed, and made a commitment to God that as soon as he began to work, he would establish a fund to give young people the opportunity to go to college. Nido made good on his commitment, creating the Nido Qubein Associates Scholarship Fund, which has provided more than $3 million in scholarships and grants to hundreds of students.

Nido had had an earlier experience of giving with no expectation of reward or return. While in junior college, he had saved

$350 to buy a car. Much to his disappointment, the cheapest vehicle he could find was $700. Nido went home to his dormitory after a discouraging day of car shopping and vented his frustration to the dorm's housemother.

When Nido's bank statement came at the end of the month, he couldn't believe his eyes. Instead of the $350 he had saved penny by penny, he saw $700 in his account! His first thought was, "The bank's made a mistake." Then he remembered his housemother. Could a woman making $200 a month from Social Security and her college stipend have put $350 in his account? When he asked her, she said simply, "I've decided it's much better for me to invest my money in the life of a budding young man than it is to park it in a savings account."

The housemother's investment paid off. Nido's life has been all about serving—professionally, personally, and philanthropically. He has chaired more companies, won more awards, written more books, headed more charitable fund-raising campaigns, and touched more lives than we have room to chronicle. Nido says, "You can't be touched by an angel and remain the same." And he didn't. In Nido's case, kindness created kindness. Service created service. And giving created giving.

Anonymous donors transcend the selfish desire for money or worldly possessions, or even the need to be recognized. They give for the sole purpose of making a difference. Every time you slip a dollar into a Salvation Army kettle, or put cash into the collection plate at church, or make an anonymous contribution to tsunami relief or rebuilding villages across the world, you are tapping into the power of transcendence.

TRANSCEND BY PAYING IT FORWARD

The book *Pay It Forward* takes the concept of making a difference to a wonderful conclusion. Trevor McKinney, a young boy, has a social studies assignment to do something that will make a positive difference in the world. Instead of paying back a favor, he decides to pay it forward: he performs good deeds for three new people. There are three criteria for each good deed: (1) it has to be something that really helps people, (2) it has to be something they can't do on their own, and (3) each one then has to perform a good deed for three new people.

Remarkable things begin to happen. People are amazed by the kindness of strangers. They, in turn, are compelled to do likewise. The movement spreads to other cities. Lives are changed as people help the homeless, give cars away, and reach out beyond themselves to do something significant and make their lives count for something greater than themselves. In essence, they learn to live in a way that transcends. And it feels good.

We too can pay good deeds forward and watch how they blossom. Whenever you take the time to mentor someone, you're paying it forward. If you give a fellow salesperson a lead to follow because you know that person is struggling, you're paying it forward. If you help out a co-worker by recommending him or her for a position or a promotion, you're paying it forward. Anytime you do something with the eye toward providing future benefits for another human being, you're paying it forward. You're following the Golden Rule, doing for others as you would like others to do for you, but with no expectation of reward on your part. The reward you receive may very well be to watch the people you have helped do the same for others in their lives. Your action can be the seed that creates a harvest of good deeds for years to come.

TRANSCEND BY LEAVING A LEGACY

Nido Qubein defines four levels at which we all live: achievement, happiness, significance, and legacy. The achievement level involves accomplishing goals, such as getting an education, starting a business, and making money. Achievement is a key ingredient to success, but the problem arises when people expect achievement alone to bring them happiness. Look at celebrities who supposedly have achieved everything they could possibly desire. To the casual onlooker, they seem to have it all—fame, fortune, and success. So why are many of their lives in shambles? Many of these so-called successful individuals struggle with drugs and alcohol or go through multiple romantic relationships. Then there are the tragic cases in which people who seem to have it all take their own lives. Could it be that these individuals thought that achievement would bring happiness and they fell into despair when it didn't? Is that true in your own life? As diligently as we all strive for achievement, is it enough?

That leads us to Nido's second level of life, the level of happiness. Without happiness, all the success in the world is meaningless. The most fulfilled people in the world recognize that happiness does not have to be tied to achievement. In fact, you're better off when you can be happy no matter what your circumstances or accomplishments.

Nido defines happiness as being "in joy," and what creates joy is different for everyone. I'm a firm believer in having as much joy as possible in life, and I'm always looking to stand guard against the forces that might try to take my joy away. But what I've also learned is that I can choose to let my joy be taken or not. Whenever something happens that might shake my joy, I shake it off instead. Happiness and joy are internal experiences that do not have to be tied to external events. It may be easier to feel joyful when your house is paid off and you got the big promotion at work and your kids are all straight-A students at the best schools. But you will truly transcend beyond your best when you can feel joy even if the mortgage is due, or you were passed over for the raise, or your kids are struggling.

Nido believes that the third level of life is significance. This is not significance in the sense of "look at me!" Instead, it is knowing that what we're doing in life really matters. In the classic film *It's a Wonderful Life*, George Bailey, who has lived in the small town of Bedford Falls all his life, comes to the end of his rope financially. Things are so bad that he decides to kill himself, thinking that then his problems will be over and his family can collect his life insurance money. That's when Clarence, the bumbling angel, shows George what Bedford Falls would have been like if George had never existed. George has a rare opportunity to see the ways he has touched people and how he has had a significant impact on many lives. It matters that George Bailey has lived. Of course, George Bailey is a fictional character—but each one of us touches the lives of others in ways we may or may not know. Everyone's life matters. It matters that you live.

According to Nido, we can know we are living significantly when we make ourselves indispensable. He says:

> . . . when considering yourself to be indispensable, it is not a condescending or braggadocious term. It's a solid term to suggest that you really ought to make sure if you're a member of a committee, you're indispensable. If you play on a sports team, you're indispensable. They can't do it without you. If you're a member of a family, you're indispensable. They need your love. They need your investment of time and energy.

Nido understands that a significant life doesn't mean having your name on a building or in lights on Broadway. It doesn't mean owning the most successful company or getting the biggest promotion or fattest bonus check. Instead, your life will be significant according to the contributions you make to others and the positive impact you make on the world. By this definition, George Bailey's life was truly significant. Whose lives have you touched? What small things have you done that made a difference to others? What can you do from this point on to live a significant life defined by the difference you have made?

When you transcend beyond your best, you can leave an indelible legacy that will inspire others long after you're gone. Leaving a legacy is Nido's fourth level of life. We will all leave a legacy, good or bad, by virtue of the fact that none

> **Every moment of life is both a gift and a moment of choice.**

of us is an island. Our lives are intertwined with the lives of others. In the same way we create significance with the smallest actions, we also can start to leave a legacy every moment by the choices we make.

Imagine that your life is one long line stretching from the moment of your birth to the moment of your death. Visualize an X on that line representing where you are now. Whether your X is close to the beginning of the line, in the middle, or closer to the end, every moment represented by that line is precious. Every moment of life is both a gift and a moment of choice. Nido Qubein says, "We transcend when we move beyond living the length of our years to living the depth and width of our years as well." What kind of legacy will you leave? How will you affect others' lives in a way that will leave the world a better place than you found it? Now is the time to start living as if each moment matters, not only for you but also for the legacy you will leave behind.

TRANSCEND BY RISING TO THE OCCASION

Sometimes we are empowered to transcend because we are faced with enormous obstacles; yet we care so much that we go beyond what we think is possible. Remember Heather, the young woman you heard about earlier in this book? Her drug-ridden life on the streets turned around when she was taken in and ultimately adopted by a caring family. Jill and Terry Mayo are the couple who welcomed Heather into their home. Rising to the occasion caused Jill and Terry to be the difference in Heather's life, even though there were great obstacles in the way.

You see, Jill and Terry's teenage daughter Claire had been using drugs, and Heather was their daughter's dealer. Whenever Heather hit bottom and needed a place to stay, Claire let her stay at the Mayo house in exchange for drugs. Jill and Terry were not aware of this arrangement. They just knew that Heather was a troubled girl, and they were glad they could offer her some help.

One rainy day, when Heather was high, sick, and seeking refuge from the streets, she went to Claire's house but found no one at home. She didn't know that the Mayos were out of town. All she knew was that she was exhausted and in need of a warm, dry place to sleep.

The front door opened easily enough; Heather only had to jiggle the handle. She walked in and headed straight to Claire's bedroom, put on a pair of her friend's pajamas, and went to sleep for three days. She got up only to make herself an occasional quesadilla, then it was back to bed. On the evening of the third day, she woke up to the sound of the front door opening. The Mayos were back. Feeling like Goldilocks about to be caught red-handed by the three bears, Heather contemplated going out the window, climbing over the fence, and coming back in the front door as if she had just arrived. But it would be hard to explain the pajamas.

So she decided to walk out and face the music. Trying to look like the cutest druggie the Mayos had ever seen, Heather walked into the living room and said hello. Understandably startled, Jill and Terry asked what she was doing there. Heather explained that she didn't have anywhere to go, so as usual she had come to their house. Fully prepared for the Mayos to call the police and have her hauled off to jail, Heather was floored when Claire's parents simply said, "We're so glad you were able to get in the house." That was when Heather began to realize the Mayos were different.

Heather didn't know that Jill and Terry were struggling with the question of what to do about her. Claire had told them about her drug problem and Heather's role as her dealer. The Mayos were trying to support Claire as she worked through her addiction, and they weren't sure about having her drug dealer in their house. But they went beyond their fears and asked, "If we are our brother's keeper, what does that mean? And what if our 'brother' is our daughter's drug dealer?"

Jill and Terry decided to view Heather simply as a girl in need of help, and they opened their home to her. "We didn't make a lot of rules at first," Jill said later. "Our theory was that we had to keep her alive long enough to get her sober. So we weren't going to worry about smoking cigarettes. We weren't going to worry about tattoos, tongue rings, eyebrow rings, weird clothes, and weird haircuts. We just made a few simple rules. No drugs. No alcohol. No sex. We had to know where she was. And she had to go to school."

The standards remained the same for ten other troubled teenage girls who filtered in and out of the Mayo home over the next two years. Jill and Terry developed a reputation in the community. Some people may have thought they were crazy, but the runaways and other girls who sought refuge with them were simply grateful for the chance. Not all of them showed it. Most of the girls came from homes where at least one parent was a drug addict, and the father usually was not in the picture. Some of the girls were pregnant. Some had been molested. Others had mental health issues. But it was clear that these teens were craving the type of care and attention they got from the Mayos.

For the next few years, the Mayo home had a revolving door. Sometimes they had so many in their home that kids were sleeping on couches. Caring for everyone's needs meant that the

Mayos had to reach into their own pockets, providing food, clothing, medical care, and even drug rehab costs. When the Mayos didn't have money, other people pitched in. Sometimes people brought them food. Sometimes people gave them money at Christmastime. Sometimes the church helped. The last child the Mayos took in stayed for three years. All this was in addition to the Mayos' own two daughters. The demands became so great that at one point Jill almost lost her job.

As their passion grew for helping kids in their community who were hurting, Jill and Terry began to have a new vision. What if they could help younger kids who hadn't yet been caught up in drugs or unplanned pregnancies? The Mayos got a foster care license and began taking in kids between the ages of seven and ten who had been abused. Tamekia moved in when she was nine and became Tamekia Mayo a year later. David was seven when the Mayos adopted him. The Mayos have worked diligently to build trust and connect to Tamekia and David. It hasn't been easy, but, according to Jill, the changes in these kids are worth every minute of the painful struggles.

At age fifty-six, with a ten-year-old and a fourteen-year-old, Jill worked full time as an accountant for a construction company. While her peers went on cruises, watched movies, and had their nails done, she was helping with homework and going to soccer games. But none of that mattered when Jill watched David score two goals in a game and remembered his first days in their home. When David arrived the Mayos made him sign a suicide contract, stating that he had to talk to Jill or his therapist if he felt as if he was going to kill himself. Now, supported by the Mayos' love, David was a completely different child.

The runaways the Mayos took in are doing equally well. Two have graduated from college, and another is in college now. Still another is in a good marriage and has a child. Another is the first woman in three generations of her family not to be pregnant at sixteen. One girl called recently to tell Jill and Terry that she has been sober for three years and is a manager at a technology company.

Jill says, "You can take the boat. You can have the summer vacations, the house on the beach. We have one car. We're not uncomfortable. We have food on the table. We are living in a way that is really satisfying." Jill and Terry Mayo have made it a way of life to invest in the lives of others in dramatic ways. They rose to the challenges presented by these young people and helped them to go far beyond their best. In doing so, they succeeded in leaving a legacy that will last forever.

TRANSCEND BY UNDERSTANDING THE REAL MEASURE OF SUCCESS

Isn't it refreshing to read stories of people who are being the difference in the world? Countless such individuals daily go beyond their best to make a positive mark that cannot be erased. When you transcend beyond your best, you too will discover the true meaning of a very common word: you'll learn the true meaning of success.

Success means something different to each and every one of us, but I'm going to go out on a limb and give you what I believe is a universal definition: *You succeed every time you do something that creates a positive effect for others.* Yes, it can create a positive effect in your life. In fact, I believe that creating a positive effect for others will inevitably benefit you. But to experience real, living, lifelong, powerful success, your efforts must benefit others. We will always do more for others than we will do for ourselves. And success is sweeter when it's shared.

Nothing can compare with the satisfaction we feel when we know we are making a positive difference in the lives of others. There is a return on your deposit of kindness. There is payback on your deposit of reaching out beyond self. We experience joy,

> **There is payback on your deposit of reaching out beyond self.**

peace, and fulfillment, knowing we have done something to be the difference.

If you haven't heard the wake-up call, here it is. It's time to answer the phone. You can go beyond your limits—whatever they are—and CONNECT. When you need to reconnect, remind yourself why it is that you are called to transcend. Then keep moving forward. Transcending never stops. Though at times the requirements may be great, the rewards of transcending far exceed the effort. You will experience a level of freedom and personal fulfillment that you have not known before. Hold onto that knowledge when challenges try their best to stop you. Remember, you can transcend beyond your best. Ralph Waldo Emerson said it best: "What lies behind us and what lies before us are tiny matters compared to what lies within us." What lies within you is the power to transcend beyond your best. What lies within you is the power to CONNECT.

TRANSCEND BEYOND YOUR BEST ACTION STEPS

1. Who are your personal heroes and examples of transcending beyond their best? Make a list of those people and why their stories have inspired you.

2. Remember a time when you truly went beyond your best and achieved something you didn't expect. If you can't think of an example, think of a time when you did a good job, and then ask, "What more could I have done to go from good to great, from better to best?" Often the effort needed to reach best and beyond is actually small. Giving a customer good service may be second nature to you.

What little thing could you do to give the customer great service?

3. What principles have you adhered to regardless of whether they caused you pain? Do you know of someone who refused to go along with the crowd even when it wasn't easy to say no? How do these examples inspire you to hold to your own principles?

4. How have you been the difference? Whose lives have you touched? Have you mentored someone? Helped a colleague at work? Given to a charity? Volunteered for a good cause? Been a role model for kids? How many ways have you been the difference, and how many other ways could you be the difference, starting now?

5. Think of an obstacle you've faced. What did you learn from adversity? How did it teach you to transcend and go beyond your best?

6. How have you demonstrated caring at home, at work, and with colleagues, friends, employees, associates, and family?

7. Where are you pursuing excellence? What could you do to raise your standards from great to excellent? What would you need to do, learn, practice, or become to be absolutely beyond the best? Where have you given from the heart?

8. What small acts of kindness have you experienced? Who has been kind to you? How did you feel? How does it feel when you are kind to others? Make a commitment to do at least one kind thing a day for others for the next week and write down how you feel when you practice kindness.

9. At least once in the next month, make an anonymous

donation to something or someone. Put a quarter in someone's parking meter. Give an extra five dollars in cash at church. Buy lunch for the person behind you in the drive-through line. Send flowers to a colleague at work. Notice how great these anonymous acts make you feel.

10. Pay at least one favor forward. Mentor someone at work. Give a co-worker a day off to be with her kids. Buy someone a copy of a book or CD that inspired you.

11. Evaluate your life on the basis of Nido Qubein's four levels. Where are you living currently? Achievement, happiness, significance, or legacy? The levels aren't mutually exclusive; you can have all four things in your life at the same time. But spend a little time each week considering the legacy you wish to leave. How do you want to be remembered? What impact do you want to have on this earth?

12. How will you rise to the occasion? How will you transcend obstacles and go beyond your best? The best way to handle obstacles is to do what you can to plan your response in advance. Looking ahead, how will you transcend the situations that we all face—loss, old age, people leaving? How will you rise above other difficulties that success might bring?

13. Based on what you've read in this book, write your own description of what success means to you. Make sure that your definition includes the positive effects you will have on others. Who will be helped when you succeed? What benefits will you and others experience? How much more will you be able to do when you act and feel successful? How will you need to transcend beyond your best to attain the level of success you just described?

14. Fill in the blank: **ICARE to take action now by being the difference and doing** _____ _____

to transcend beyond my best.

Conclusion
CONNECT to the BE-Attitudes

In all that you get, get understanding.
—*Proverbs 4:7*

We started this book with the proposition that CONNECT is a framework for both personal and professional success. Chapter by chapter, we've built that framework, one support at a time. On its own, each beam is powerful and able to uphold you as you encounter various challenges, undergo change, and strive to realize visions and goals. Put all the beams together and you have a completed framework, which when embedded in the foundation of your life will support whatever you choose to build upon it. Not only that, it will withstand the storms that will inevitably blow your way.

This book is your blueprint. Within it lie all the tools for overcoming the limits of your beliefs so you realize how great you can be. You can go from better to best and then beyond your best. You can become the best you can possibly become, moment by moment, day by day, week by week, month by month, and season by season. With the BE-Attitudes as your foundation, you can maintain a continuous improvement process 365 days a year, overcoming complacency, mediocrity, and yesterday's excuses.

Incorporate the BE-Attitudes into your life, and you will build upon your current and future successes.

THE CONNECT STEPS AND BE-ATTITUDES THAT BUILD SUCCESS

Commit to win.	**BE** accountable.
Open up to opportunities.	**BE** a change embracer.
Notice what's needed and do what's necessary.	**BE** aware.
Navigate by your purpose.	**BE** vision centered.
Execute ethically: Do what's right because it's right.	**BE** performance and integrity driven.
Challenge your challenges.	**BE** responsible.
Transcend beyond your best.	**BE** the difference.

The BE-Attitudes will enable you to connect to your dreams, goals, purpose, and overall success in life. We're not saying it's going to be easy. We're not saying at times we may all feel disconnected. We're not saying sometimes you may feel actively disengaged. It's okay when you miss the mark. Just get back up and dust yourself off. If you miss it again, get back up and keep trying until you get it right. CONNECT is a process. It starts with going to the BE-Attitudes and reminding yourself of what you can be. You can BE accountable. You can BE a change embracer. You can BE aware. You can BE vision centered. You can BE performance and integrity driven. You can BE responsible. You can BE the difference.

You can be all of those things by practicing the behaviors discussed throughout this book. As you do so, you must continually repeat the truth that all things are possible to those who believe. You can tap into an even greater potential than you knew you had. What resides inside of you is greater than the opposing forces outside of you.

Remember, CONNECT starts and ends with people, purpose, and performance. Your success will come from connecting with all three at the deepest possible level, from creating and following a vision that goes beyond you and your own needs, that includes helping others to win as well. Continue to think, speak, and act like the winner you are, and you will begin to live this higher vision of yourself. Know that you are unique, born with a purpose, and predestined for greatness. Once you connect to those truths, you will begin to thrive. You will be on a course of continuous improvement that will lead you to success. The dreams you have for yourself, your organization, your team, or your family, will start to become a reality.

At the end of my talks on CONNECT, I ask my audiences to turn and connect with the person sitting next to them. Then I tell them when the music comes on to jump up out of their seats. We do a countdown—"Three, two, one, HIT THE MUSIC!" The music comes up and everyone leaps to his feet. All running around the room, giving double-high-fives to everyone they meet, looking one another straight in the eye as they say, "You're going UP!"

That's exactly what you're ready to do. Imagine you hear the music as you leap to your feet, ready to take on the world. I double-high-five you as we tell each other, "You're going UP!"

Building success through people, purpose, and performance. CONNECT!

ACKNOWLEDGMENTS

I was again blessed to have the help and support of many wonderful people to whom I want to express an attitude of gratitude.

To Marion Maneker, my editor, Sarah Brown, and the other super fantastic HarperCollins staff.

To my literary agent, Jan Miller, Shannon Miser-Marven, Cheri Gillis, and the entire team for their ongoing confidence and support.

To Marsha Cansler, and Victoria St. George of Just Write, for your outstanding skills, wisdom, and professionalism and, oh yes, for your countless hours. I thank God for both of you.

To Hattie Hill, my friend and mentor, special thanks for your love, insight, and valuable contribution to this book.

And finally, to the many individuals who contributed to make this book a reality! Amie Brooks, Jennifer Canzoneri, Donna Cash, Dr. Cherry Collier, Cassie Glasgow, Arabella Grayson, Sam Horn, Joycelyn Fannin, Cherlond Lofton, James Pagano, Hue Tran, Lisa Hobbs, Wanda E. Moorman, Michele Rubino, Janet Wagner, and the entire SpeakersOffice, Inc. management team.